Covington's
German Heritage

Don Heinrich Tolzmann

HERITAGE BOOKS
2008

HERITAGE BOOKS

AN IMPRINT OF HERITAGE BOOKS, INC.

Books, CDs, and more—Worldwide

For our listing of thousands of titles see our website
at
www.HeritageBooks.com

Published 2008 by
HERITAGE BOOKS, INC.
Publishing Division
100 Railroad Ave. #104
Westminster, Maryland 21157

International Standard Book Numbers
Paperbound: 978-0-7884-1059-8
Clothbound: 978-0-7884-7082-0

Table of Contents

Covington, a new town, is laid out at the mouth of the Licking River, on the farm lately owned by Mr. Thomas Kennedy. This commanding & beautiful situation is generally known throughout the Western country, situated at the confluence of Ohio and Licking Rivers, in Campbell County, Kentucky, opposite to the flourishing town of Cincinnati. This situation presents a prospect equal if not superior to any on the Ohio River; the main road from Lexington, Ky. To Cincinnati, Dayton, and western parts of the state of Ohio passes through the town, it is healthy and possesses many advantages superior to any situation in the Western country, convenient to a good market, steam mill, and a variety of factories, the facility with which all kinds of building materials can be procured with many other concomitant advantages, must hold forth sufficient inducements for the enterprising merchant, mechanic, manufacturer & men of business of every description.

The Western Spy (1815)

Covington's Germans have participated in the development of the city in outstanding ways. Even today they still lead great business enterprises. They were the most zealous advocates of the new monumental buildings that adorn the city, such as the court house, for example. In terms of politics, they were a factor that cannot be underestimated and a group that does not let itself be carried along by every current, even when others become weak-kneed. As public officials, Germans also enjoy the confidence of their fellow citizens, and German honesty and uprightness are still proverbial today.

Gedenkblatt zum 25-jaehrigen Jubilaeums des Deutschen Pionier-Vereins von Covington, KY (1902)

v

Preface

Covington, Kentucky is located directly in the middle of the Greater Cincinnati metropolitan area, which historically is known as one of the three major centers of German-American heritage, along with St. Louis and Milwaukee. Due to its location at the center of this metropolitan area, Covington is often overlooked, as it is an integral part of the area in a social, cultural and economic sense. If Cincinnati is the Queen City of the west, then Covington, Kentucky is certainly second only to her in rank. However, this should not obscure the history of Covington, nor that of its German heritage. Although the German heritage of Cincinnati has been covered in a variety of works, there was no up-to-date survey for that of Covington, Kentucky, and this work aims to fill that gap.

Don Heinrich Tolzmann
University of Cincinnati

Introduction

In preparing this work, it was my intention to complete an introduction to the history of Covington's German heritage. However, in the process of completing the work, it soon became apparent that the work served a twofold purpose. First, it of course, aims to provide a survey history of the topic, which will be of interest to those in the area. However, it also accomplishes another second purpose, in that it conveys the story of the German-American experience by means of the example of the Covington Germans. And, in this sense, the work will be of interest and use elsewhere.

Although the history of each and every German-American community across the country is in and of itself unique, they all shared some common ground in terms of the kinds of experiences that they had. This history covers the period of the German pioneers, immigration, settlement, the establishment of various trades and industries, the building of the community, the introduction of German social life, customs, and values, the confrontation with nativism in the 19th and 20th centuries, and the German heritage today.

In editing, this volume, I have aimed to utilize German-language source materials whenever possible. Chapters 1-3, hence, consist of my translations of three articles by H. A. Rattermann, which were based on lectures he presented at meetings of the German Pioneer Society of Covington in 1877.[1] In the following chapters, I have tried to bring the story up-to-date to the present time. I have also included appendices with references to some of the major points of interest in relation to the German heritage of Covington, and also a list of the founding members of the German Pioneer Society.

It is the editor's hope that this volume will contribute to an understanding of German-American history in general and of Covington's German heritage in particular, and that it will also provide a foundation for future work in the area. There are many aspects and dimensions of Covington's German heritage, which are deserving of further exploration, and hopefully this work will provide the convenient point of departure.

In conclusion, several acknowledgments are in order. I would like to thank Charles D. King, Local History Librarian, Kenton County Public Library, for assistance in the location of materials in his library. Also, thanks to other members of the library, who were also of assistance.[2] I would also like to thank Thomas H. Leech, Department of Literature and Language, Northern Kentucky University, for his translation of the history of the German Pioneer Society of Covington, which appears as Chapter 5. Thanks to Paul A. Tenkotte, Thomas Moore College, for information he provided about the German churches of Covington. Thanks also to Ralph Murray, Cincinnati, who provided me with some useful information and references to various aspects of Covington's German heritage, and, finally, gratitude is expressed to Dorothy Young, Department of Germanic Languages and Literatures, University of Cincinnati, for the preparation of the manuscript of this work.

DHT

Notes

1. H. A. Rattermann, "Die deutschen Pioniere von Kenton County, Kentucky," *Der Deutsche Pionier*. 9(1877): 258-64, 309-15, 352-57.

2. A wealth of materials on the history of Northern Kentucky can be found at the Kenton County Public Library, as well as a collection of paintings by Frank Duveneck, the major German-American artist of the region.

Chapter 1

The German Pioneers Before 1810

Introduction - Covington & Newport older than Cincinnati - The first owner of land in Covington a German - The Royal American Battalion - Captain Heinrich Bouquet - German Soldiers - Gerhard Muse's Land in Covington - Kennedy's Ferry - The Founding of Covington - General Leonard Covington - Street Names - Growth and Development of the City -Failed Speculation - Jäger and Sträter - Captain Harrod's Company - The Sodowsky Brothers - Hinkson's Party - Edmund Rittenhaus - The first Marriage in Kenton County - The first child in Covington - Georg Michael Bedinger - Johannes Piper - Other Germans before 1810.

**

Covington is the youngest sister of the group of cities located midway on the Ohio River, of which the oldest carries the grand title, "Queen of the West." Even if Covington is the youngest, it certainly is not the least of them. And, even if it were not standing as it were in the shadow of the greater and larger city of Cincinnati, then it certainly would still be counted as one of the most important cities of the region.[1]

Is it not the second largest city of Kentucky with a population of ca. 30,000 (1877) and with an estimated total wealth of more than 25 million dollars? However, as a result of the fact that it is a quasi suburb of Cincinnati, the importance of the city of Covington recedes, and Covington must content itself by basking in the reflected glory of its more powerful sister across the Ohio River.[2]

1

Hence, Covington forms an integral part of the substantial commerce of the great capital city of the Ohio Valley, and its history becomes only a part of the history of this great metropolis. Therefore, it is rendered even more difficult to write a history of the city, because so many interesting aspects and episodes are part and parcel of the history of the area. Nevertheless, I will attempt to do so, and if I fail to achieve this goal, then I hope that I will not be harshly judged for having tried to attain this objective.[3]

I have often heard the opinion that Covington or Newport are older than Cincinnati, but this is an error. Cincinnati was laid out in 1789-90, in the first year under the name "Losantiville" and in the later under its present name, but Newport dates from 1796 and Covington from 1815. One of the reasons for this mistake may well be that the land south of the Ohio River was placed on the market at an earlier date than that north of the river. The first land warrants, or patents, north of the Ohio, were taken out in 1788, whereas warrants for lands in Kentucky were drawn up in the province of Virginia as early as 1763. And, this brings us to the theme of the pioneers of the Licking Valley.

It is noteworthy that the first owner of property not only in Covington, but in Kenton County as well, was a German. When the French and Indian War broke out in 1754, and which ended in 1763 with the acquisition of New France, i.e. Canada, and the Ohio Valley by England, a German regiment was formed in the German province of Hannover, which at that time was connected to England by means of the royal family.

This unit, the Royal American, or 62nd regiment, was sent to America and landed in Philadelphia in December

2

1756. As the pox had broken out on board ship, the commandant, Captain Heinrich Bouquet had a difficult time locating quarters for the troops.[4]

This led to problems between the government officials and authorities of the city who did not want to recognize the requisition of the Quartermaster of the Battalion, Friederich Tulleken.[5] However, as this does not belong to the topic under consideration, we shall mention this only in passing. It should be noted that the regiment consisted predominantly of Germans, but mixed with a few Dutchmen and Swiss. They had served in the military campaigns in Flanders, and had been enticed to come to America with the promise of 200 acres of land in the Ohio Valley in addition to salary.[6]

Amongst these soldiers, there was a certain Gerhard Muse, who at the conclusion of the war in 1763, received 200 acres (land warrant 367), which was in accordance with the royal proclamation, in Kentucky, which at that time was a distant county of the state of Virginia. Muse located his property on the land forming the southwest corner of the confluence of the Licking and Ohio Rivers.[7]

However, he did not take possession of the land, and after having merely located it on the map, he traded it off for a barrel of brandy to another, who also apparently placed little value on it, and traded it to James Taylor of Virginia "for a few pounds of buffalo meat." Taylor then traded the land to Stephan Trigg, who sold it to John Todd, Jr. The land then passed to James Welsh.

Muse's land patent is dated: 14 February 1780 by the office of the Governor of Virginia, Beverley Randolph; Welsh's document is dated: 20 September 1787. Hence,

3

these land titles date from a time period before any land titles for the territory north of the Ohio River. Stephan Trigg, who was referred to above, had arrived in Kentucky as a land surveyor, and perished in the Battle of Blue Licks, 19 August 1782.[8]

None of these owners settled on their land in Kentucky, as it was not until one of the pioneers of Cincinnati, Thomas Kennedy, arrived and purchased the land in 1792, that the land was actually settled on. The property stretched from the Licking river to approximately the location of today's Philadelphia St., and to the south to about somewhere past 8th St.

Due to the steady commerce and trade between Lexington and the major metropolis of the West at that time, namely Cincinnati, Kennedy established a ferry boat business in 1795 for traffic across the Ohio River. As a result, Covington became known as "Kennedy's Ferry."

It retained the name until 1815, when two brothers, General John S. and Richard M. Gano together with Thomas Carneal purchased 150 acres of Kennedy's farm for $50,000, and laid out the town of Covington.

The following served as trustees for the sale of lots in the city: Alfred Sanford; John C. Buckner, a Pennsylvania German; Uriel Sebree; John Hudson; and Joseph Kennedy. the city laid out by them stretched from the Licking to the vicinity of Russel St., and south to 8th St. However, lots were only laid out east to Washington St., and north to 6th St.

The name of the city was derived from General Leonard Covington (Kurfingthan), who was born 30 October

4

1768 in Aquasco, Prince County, Maryland. His father had settled there in the mid-18th century, and came from a knightly family from the Department of the Upper Alsace in the vicinity of Neu-Breisbach. Written documents from the family (1697) indicate that the family name was written as Korfinghthan, or Kurfingthan.

Covington's father had come to America as an officer with a French military unit. After he had been captured, was brought to Maryland, where he eventually settled and married. Here his name was anglicized into the more readily pronounceable "Covington," while at the same time the name was eventually Frenchified in the Alsace as "Cocqfontaine."[9]

General Covington was appointed a lieutenant of the dragoons, 14 March 1792, and was ordered to serve on an expedition of General Anthony Wayne to the Maumee. In the battles at Fort Recovery and Fallen Timbers he clearly demonstrated his bravery, for which Wayne cited him for special commendation in his report. Thereupon, he was promoted to the rank of captain in 1794, after which he resigned military service and settled down on his farm. Due to its mills, it became known as "French Mills." He served several times in the state legislature of Maryland, and was elected to Congress in 1805.

In 1809, he became lieutenant-col. of a calvary regiment, and in 1813 rose to the rank of brigadier general. Due to the War of 1812 with Great Britain, he was then commanded to proceed to the Canadian border, and was wounded in the battle at Chrysler's Field, 12 February 1813, and died two days later. Covington was considered one of the most competent officers and soldiers in the U. S. Army.[10]

The streets in Covington received their name from the governors of Kentucky: Isaac Shelby; James Garrard; Christopher Greenup, a Virginia German (Grönup); Charles Schott; and George Madison. Also, names came from the previous owner of the land: Thomas Kennedy and General Thomas Sandford, the first member of Congress from the region. Cross streets were numbered from one to six.

The city grew slowly, and the 1830 U.S. Census showed that there was a population of 715. The speculators who had originally laid out the city, had a difficult time with their investment, as they had not sold a great deal of the lots. At first, due to the excitement and interest in the area, however, a number of lots had been sold, and this saved them from bankruptcy. Fifteen years later, many of the lots sold for half the original price.

These early investors tried in vain to promote the growth and development of the city, making use of all kinds of imaginable ideas. Hence, in 1828, a company was formed for the purpose of constructing a bridge across the Ohio River, and was incorporated by the Kentucky state legislature, 29 January 1829. Also, on 27 June 1830, a company was incorporated to build a railway from Covington to Lexington. The lack of *nervus rerum*, however, caused both projects to be postponed. Covington really only began to grow and develop after the 1830s due to two factors: first, it was incorporated as a city, 24 February 1834. Second the German immigration to the area increased substantially in the 1830s.

The first Germans in Kenton County were: George Jäger and Johannes Strader, or Sträter, who together with Simon Kenton, explored the Licking River in the fall of 1771. Only a few years later, in May 1774, several Virginia

6

Germans arrived: Jacob Harrod, Abraham Hite (Heit), Jakob and Joseph Sodowsky, and 38 others.[11] They came down the Ohio River, and landed at the mouth of the Licking River, and felled the first trees at Deer Creek, where they made their camp.

The two Sodowsky brothers, usually referred to as Sandusky, lived for a while in Campbell County, and were of an adventurous nature. They had come from Strassburg, Virginia for the purpose of seeking their fortunes in the Wild West. In the fall 1775, Jacob Sodowsky traveled from Harrod's settlement to the Cumberland River, purchased a canoe and then went down the Ohio River to the Mississippi, and then further on down to New Orleans. From there, he took a ship to Baltimore, and made his way back to Virginia, and then returned to Kentucky in the following year. He then built Sandusky Station in Washington County at Pleasant Run with his brother.

Jakob then settled in Campbell County, but moved to Jefferson County, where he died, whereas his brother died in Bourbon County.[12] Jakob was the first European American (exclusive of the French and Spanish) to travel down the Ohio River all the way to New Orleans. Sandusky County, Ohio is named for the father of the two brothers, as are the two cities of Upper and Lower Sandusky, and the Sandusky River in Ohio. Their father, Johann Sodowsky, was an ethnic German from Posen, Poland, who had come to America in the mid-18th century. He established a trading business based in Detroit, which dealt with the Indians in Ohio. A tradition station of his in Ohio, Sandusky, became well known, and the name was also accepted by the Indians.[13]

The first European Americans, however, to traverse the Licking River were in the so-called Hinkson party: Johannes Hinkson, Johann Hagen (Haggin), Johann Müller, and 12 others. they came down the Ohio River in March-April 1771, and then traveled down the Licking River in search of land suitable for a settlement.[14]

One of the first settlers in Kenton County was Edmund Rittenhaus, also known in the anglicized spelling as Rittenhouse. He was a relative of the famous German-American astronomer and scientist David Rittenhouse. He came down the Ohio River in March 1793, and landed in Cincinnati, and then traveled down the Licking, and settled at the confluence with the Banklick River. However, due to the hostility of the Indians, he stayed at Ruddel's Station, located between Paris and Cynthiana. He returned in 1795, and settled on the west side of the Licking River, about 3 miles below Three Mile Ripple.[15]

About a quarter of a mile from there, Johannes Martin settled down at approximately the same time, in the vicinity of Buena Vista. He came from Beesontown, Pennsylvania, and was a Quaker. His son Wilhelm Martin, married Margaretha Rittenhaus in 1797, the daughter of Edmund Rittenhaus, and this is considered the first marriage in Kenton County. A son was born to this couple, Isaac Martin, 4 May 1798, who is considered to be the first European American born in Kenton County. He lived in the hilly area south of Covington, in the vicinity of the railway tunnels.

Georg Michael Bedinger, who in April 1779 had been part of the expedition of Captain Johann Baumann (Bowman) against the Shawnee villages in the area of what is today Chillicothe, also settled down in Kenton County. His descendants lived in Covington. A son, Benjamin F. Bedinger, lived at Lexington Pike, and died in 1875 at an old age.[16]

Johannes Piper, a north German, whose parents had settled in the Savannah area in 1742, came to Kenton County, where he bought a trace of land from John Rogers (parcel no. 7093) consisting of 3,546 ½ acres. Of this, he sold 1,541 acres to Charles Morgan.[17]

Other early Germans, who came to Kenton County before 1810 were: Stephan Reich, Franz Kreilich, Jakob Kraut, Abraham Rockenfeld, Jakob Holmann. Also, another early settler was Jan Van Hook, a Dutchman.[18]

Notes

1. For a general guide to the history of the Greater Cincinnati area, see Geoffrey J. Giglierano et al, *The Bicentennial Guide to Greater Cincinnati: A Portrait of Two Hundred Years*, (Cincinnati: Cincinnati Historical Society, 1988). With regard to Covington in particular, see Paul Allen Tenkotte, "Rival Cities to Suburb: Covington and Newport, Kentucky, 1790-1890," (Ph.D. Diss., University of Cincinnati, 1989) and Allen Webb Smith, *Beginning at "The Point": A Documented History of Northern Kentucky and Environs, The Town of Covington in Particular, 1751-1834.* (Park Hills, Ky.: Smith, 1977).

2. For a brief survey of Covington, see Giglierano, pp. 122-37.

3. For a biography of Rattermann, see Mary Edmund Spanheimer, *Heinrich Armin Rattermann, German-American Author, Poet, and Historian, 1832-1923.* (Washington, D. C.: The Catholic University of America, 1937).

4. The Royal American Regiment consisted of four battalions, each of which consisted of a thousand men. Although originally drawn from soldiers in Germany, once in America, the Regiment drew on recruits from the soldiers in Germans in Pennsylvania. See Don Heinrich Tolzmann, ed., *The German-American Soldier: J. G. Rosengarten's Survey.* (Bowie, Maryland: Heritage Books, Inc., 1996), pp. 16-22.

5. See the *Colonial Records of Pennsylvania.* Vol. VIII, pp. 358-78 and *Pennsylvania Archives.* Vol. III, pp. 82, 85, and 111, where this conflict is discussed.

10

6. "At the commencement of the Seven Years War, in 1754, Governor Dinwiddie, of Virginia, to stimulate enlistments, issued a proclamation, granting two thousand acres of land on the Ohio to officers and soldiers. This grant was afterwards confirmed by the King." See, C. W. Butterfield, ed., *The Washington Letters-Crawford Letters*. (Cincinnati: Robert Clarke & Co., 1877), p.11.

7. A son of Muse's, Captain W. Muse, served in the 1st Maryland Battalion in the American Revolution and was later a member of the Order of Cincinnati. See, James McSherry, *A History of Maryland.* (Baltimore: J. Murphy & Co., 1850).

8. See Lewis Collins, *Collins' Historical Sketches of Kentucky,* 2 ed. (Covington, Ky.: Collins & Co., 1874, Vol. II, 427.

9. See *Armorial de la Generalite D'Alsace*. (Paris, Colmar & Strassburg, 1861), p. 280.

10. See Francis S. Drake, *Dictionary of American Biography.* Boston: J. R. Osgood & Co., 1872), p. 224.

11. Hite was a grandson of the first settler of the Shenandoah Valley in Virginia, Jost Heit. He settled down in 1732 by Opequon, which is about five miles south of Winchester, along with his sons and son-in-laws Georg Baumann, Jacob Christmann and Paul Fromann. See Samuel Kercheval, *A History of the Valley of Virginia*. 2 ed. (Woodstock, Va.: J. Gatewood, 1850), p.41. For further information on the migration of the Virginia Germans to Kentucky, see Hermann Schuricht, *The German Element in Virginia: Hermann Schuricht's History*. Edited by Don Heinrich Tolzmann. (Bowie, Maryland: Heritage Books, Inc., 1993).

12. Jacob Sodowsky maintained a diary, which however, was lost by a printer, who had intended on printing it. In 1843, there were still two sons of Joseph Sodowsky, twin brothers, living in Cincinnati. *American Pioneer*. II, pp. 325-26.

13. Regarding the early German immigration and settlement in Ohio, see, Emil Klauprecht, *German Chronicle in the History of the Ohio Valley and its Capital City, Cincinnati, in Particular*. Translated by Dale V. Lally and edited by Don Heinrich Tolzmann. (Bowie, Maryland: HeritageBooks, Inc., 1992).

14. Collins, II, p. 325.

15. Regarding Rittenhouse, see Edward Ford, *David Rittenhouse, Astronomer-Patriot, 1732-1796*. (Philadelphia: University of Pennsylvania Press, 1946) and Daniel Kolb Cassel, *A Genea-Biographical History of the Rittenhouse Family and all its Branches in America, with Sketches of their Descendants, from the Earliest Available Records to the Present Time*. (Philadelphia: the Rittenhouse Memorial Association, 1893).

16. Regarding Bedinger, see Klauprecht, pp. 95, 120.

17. See the land register of Campbell County, Vol. 1, p. 27.

18. For further references to the German pioneers of Kentucky, see Klauprecht, pp. 65-69.

Chapter 2

German Immigration and Settlement to 1850

New Settlers - Peter Schinkel - Philipp Busch - The
Descendants of Johann Mardis - The Wolf Brothers -
Covington becomes a City - The first Mayor - The County
Seat - The First County Court - Judge Louis Klette - The
Court House - Music Teacher Hermann Heinrich Plumann -
Pioneer Innkeepers - In Praise of Inns - Karl Brosemer,
Michael Linger, Friedrich Perdeszet - Michael Ufheil,
Rudolph Menke & Co. - Rising Sun Hotel - A Drink Table -
Karl Geisbauer's Brewery - Germans in Covington in the
1840s.

***

Between 1810 and 1825, more German settlers arrived
in Covington, among them: Peter Schinkel, the father of
Vincent and Amos Schinkel (Shinkle), president of the
Cincinnati and Covington Bridge Co. Mr. Schinkel, sen., was
81 years of age as of today (1877).[1] At the same time, Philipp
Busch from Mannheim, Germany settled in Covington. His
son, Eduard S. Busch, had a tavern on 4th St. by Willow Run,
where Mr. Deglow later resided.

Johann Mardis must have also settled in Covington at
about the same time. When he died in 1825, he left behind
three sons: Wilhelm, Johann, and Joseph, as well as a farm of
45 acres, of which Johann sold his share to Wilhelm for $25.
A bill of sale, however, was not drawn up and when Johann
died in 1840 and left a minor child, his brother Wilhelm had
to issue an appeal to the court to validate his title to the land,

at which time he indicated he was a German and not familiar with the laws. Thereupon, the court appointed a commissioner to legally execute the transfer of the title to him. The costs were twice the amount he had paid for the land.[2]

Another settler of this time period was a veteran of the American Revolution, Johannes Kern, who settled in Kenton County in 1823; he died 5 October 1840. The brothers Jakob and Karl Wolf from Mannheim, Germany also came to Covington at about the same time. Karl had a plumbing business for many years at 5th St., between Scott and Madison. The Wolf's were well to do and owned a large piece of property in the southeast corner of Covington, which they laid out in lots. This area is still known as Wolf's subdivision.[3]

As noted earlier, Covington became a city in 1834, and Mortimer M. Benton was elected the first mayor. Thereafter, Covington gradually began to grow and develop, and in 1840 already had a population of 2,026. In that year, Kenton County was separated from Campbell County by law and elevated to the rank of a separate court district with Independence as its capital. One, however, should not imagine that this city was especially large or attractive by any means. In 1870, its population numbered only 134. there was one straught street and another crossing it with a dozen or so miserable homes clustered around them, as well as a few taverns, where one could get some tough beef, or a piece of picled ham with boiled potatoes together with bad buttermilk, and even worse whiskey. Moreover, one could not even find a glass of beer, or wine there. That is Independence, the capital city of Kenton County, the third wealthiest county in Kentucky!

When I was there a few months ago, and lodged in one of the hotels, I noticed the unwashed children of the Irish landlady were laying around the place along with the house rooster and hen, dog and cat, in a rather discomforting array on the floor of the dining room. And, a mother pig with her suckling babies was stretched snorting and grunting across the doorway, as if it was also a guest at the hotel, and was waiting to be invited to the table. I was, hence, not in the least surprised by the quality of the food at this hotel in the county seat of Kenton County, even though I had just arrived and was tired from the trip. Could it have been like this on 4 March 1840 when the first court session was held in the home of Elias Williams in Bagley precinct?

The first legal action undertaken by the court, after the appropriate county officials had been appointed and sworn in, (among them: Leonard Stephans as sheriff, William A. Pendleton as county recorder, and Wilhelm Hoffmann as street commissioner) was the approval of a liquor license to Eduard Butz.[4] At that time, he had a tavern in Covington at Lexington Pike. Butz was a German, and the father of the infamous Know-Nothing marshall, Clinton Butts. In the Know-Nothing conflict with the German-American Turners in 1856, Butts suffered a broken arm.[5]

After the above mentioned court actions, the court adjourned, and on the 19th of May met again at the church at Bank Lick. In the meantime, John McCallum offered the court five acres of land in Independence for the public buildings of the county, an offer which was accepted with gratitude. Thereupon, the justice of peace, Louis Klette, a German immigrant who was a surveyor, was commissioned to survey two acres of this land, the sale of which would provide the necessary funds for the construction of a court house.[6] Klette was also appointed the first treasurer of Kenton County, 21 June 1841, a position he held until 20 November 1843, when Robert Carlisle was elected as his successor.

The new court house was built on the gift piece of property, but the builder apeared not to have learned as much as other journeymen in the trade. After building a cabinet, other journeymen ask their master builders "Master, the cabinet is ready now, shall I fix it?" The court house had just moved into the new building, when it decided on 21 February 1842 that C. W. Huls should undertake repairs on the building to prevent rain from coming through the bell tower, and for which adequate compensation would be provided.

Earlier, I asked by implication the question as to whether the county seat was always such a sorry little nest, as it is today, and will now proceed as preachers do, to answer the question, which none of the parishioners do during a sermon. To judge by the court records, Independence appears to have been a more agreeable place that it is today, because on 21 November 1843 Hermann Heinrich Plumann received permission from the court to conduct weekly music classes with brass and string instruments in one of the court rooms.[7] It must have been a lively and joyful time when the musicians of Independence played in the halls of the sacred *Themis* under the direction of a German conductor, who it should also be noted was the school master.

In order that the musicians could again play their instruments after a hard day of blowing them to the point of becoming dry and parched, a certain German came to their rescue to quench their thirst. Johannes Hoffmann, an innkeeper, settled down in Independence as one ready, willing and able to be of service. In 1842, the court granted him a liquor license. As a result, one could now find a good glass of beer, or wine in the county seat.

In Covington, there was no such concern, as there was a number of German innkeepers and grocers: Karl Brosemer, Michael Lingers, Friedrich Perdeszet, Michael Ufheil, and Oskar H. Conrad. And so that the innkeepers did not run out of brew, Karl Geisbauer was always hard at work in his brewery to prepare the beverage discovered by King Gambrinus for those who are thirsty.[8]

At this point, further information is in order regarding these German pioneer innkeepers and brewers of Covington, because such people who serve at the altar of Bachus and at the throne of Gambrinus are not the usual kind of people, but are really benefactors of those dying of thirst - the anchor of hope for all dry tongues and pallettes.[9]

And the star on the sign above their door beams brightly to the thristy wanderer on the road just like the North Star shines forth to the sailor, leading him safely to his port, where he can refresh himself after having survived going without the brew for some tome. Be it wine or beer, the innkeepers rightly know that they will work from morning to night to be of service to their fellow man!

We Germans may sing a song of praise to our innkeepers and brewers, because we are, it should be noted, at all times moderate in our consumption, if not more moderate than any other people in the world. We do not conceal the fact that we enjoy our beverages, but do so publicly and honorably. We are not like the sanctimonious hyprocrites who wrinkle their brow with puritanical expressions, except when it is dark and no one can see but owls and cats, carry on their wild orgies - poeple like that hold thier hands over their eyes if they see the knee of a three year old in public, but are all too ready to spend money to see the navel of a twenty-three year old in private.

No, we Germans have no love for the dark side of life, we are open and honest! Those hypocrites are the kind of people for whom consumption in private is the greatest pleasure. I know, for example, someone for whom the hardest crust of bread nibbled on in private was more tasty than the finest tortes and pastries.

However, we Germans are not nibblers, we eat and drink that which tastes good to us, and we are not concerned who sees us. We are also not afraid of our wives in the way the puritanical hypocrites are. For example, we do not regard it a sin to drink a glass of beer at home. Moreover, womenfolk, wives and daughters are an integral part of our social life, and enjoy life as we do - all honorably together! Therefore, German-American societies are honorable and upright organizations, as women participate fully. This makes social life happier and more normal than if only men are present.

Our inns are not merely bars, but rather social places of conversation and entertainment, where many an informative and edifying word has been spoken in the context of a friendly group. Many important and beneficial projects have begun in a German-American inn. Churches, schools, and societies, especially in America, are often indebted to a society, which originally met in an inn, or grocery, gathered at a table, or around a keg. Hence, many innkeepers are also preachers and school masters at the same time, and a table at an inn is often a more effective pulpit than that of a church, and a more successful podium than that of a university. and politics - what better place to be discussed than in an inn? And, as far as the news of the day goes - what better place to discuss than in the rooms of an inn?

Truly, the innkeepers are apostles and missionaries, and, hence, we cannot underestimate their services, but rather must make the work of these pioneers known, just as we praise that of the other German pioneers. However, with all humor now aside, we must say that without innkeepers and inns much would not have taken place and many a pioneer experience could not have been told and recorded had it not been preserved and retold at one of our inns. However, now back to our history.

Karl Brosemer's grocery, or inn was across from the court house. Brosemer, who came in the 1820s to Covington, was also a baker, and later moved to Ludlowtown, where he also had a nursery, and died in the 1850s. He was the father-in-law of Uncle Joe Siefert in Cincinnati, who was a frequent visitor in Covington. Broesemer's inn was a meeting place for the German Catholics of Covington in the early 1840s, and it was here that Father Kühr won a following, which led to the founding of the first German Catholic congregation of Covington.[10]

Michael Linger's inn, the Covington Exchange, was located at Greenup St., between 2nd and 3rd St. Linger was a Bavarian, and had one of the most fashionable saloons in town.

Friedrich Perdeszet, who was from Lorraine, had an inn on Greenup St., between 3rd St. and the lower market.

Michael Ufheil was the first German hotel landlord in Covington. He was from Baden and had come to Cincinnati in the early 1830s, where he was occupied as a porter at the Broadway Hotel. Then he became a waiter in George Selve's Bank Exchange located in the 3rd St. in Cincinnati, and later served in the same capacity in Michael Linger's saloon in Greenup St., located in the vicinity of the court house. In 1841 or 1842 he built the Rising Sun Tavern on Lexington Pike, between Riddle and Kydd St. This was the first building constructed on Lexington Pike. Ufheil later passed away in Newport. In the court and property records his name is entered in various forms: Uffal, Affal, Offal, and Oaffal.[11] Michael Ufheil's brother, Joseph A. Ufheil, acquired a home at the corner of Starr St. and Lexington Pike, 5 October 1844.

The inns of that time seem to have taken pleasure in the rising sun as a motif, because as early as 1839 Rudolph Menke and Co. opened a hotel and inn with that name. This Rising Sun Hotel was located on Greenup St. However, I cannot say whether the hosts of the hotel served their guests in accordance with the time of day as they do in Northern California, and as was reported by Charles Nordhoff.[12] In his work, he makes mention of the so-called "Toddy Time-Table" with the following kinds of offerings:

Toddy Drink Table

6 a.m., an Eye Opener
7 a.m., an Appetizer
8 a.m., a Digester
9 a.m., a Calmer
10 a.m., a Refresher
11 a.m., a Stimulant
12 p.m., a Pre-Luncher

1 p.m., a Topper-Offer
2 p.m., an Energizer
3 p.m., a Mender
4 p.m., a Socializer
5 p.m., an Enlivener
6 p.m., a Hardy Clear One
7 p.m., a Chatterer
8 p.m., a Laugher
9 p.m., an Uplooker
10 p.m., a Fizzer
11 p.m., an Enthuser
12 a.m., a Nightcap
Good Night!

As the sun rises in the summer in Covington at 5 a.m., and as the innkeepers arise at the same time, then perhaps the list should be amended to include another item at this time: a Waker-Upper!

Conrad obtained a liquor license on 21 December 1846 for an inn, but nothing more is known of his place. On the other hand, Karl Geisbauer, the pioneer beer brewer of the Ohio Valley, is quite well known. Born in Lorenzen, in the district of Zabern, Department Lower Rhine in the Alsace, he came to Germantown, Ohio in 1830. His cousin, Philipp Schleich, had arrived there from Philadelphia in the 1820s, and had opened up a brewery. Geisbauer opened one up there also in 1828. Germantown it should be noted was founded by Philipp Gunkel.[13] Schleich is noteworthy for brewing the first summer beer in the USA!

After residing in Germantown for seven years, Geisbauer moved to Cincinnati, where he became foreman in the brewery of Conrad Schultz, and remained there until

1842. In the meantime, Jonte and Walker had opened a brewery in Covington, which had not been profitable, and was closed, whereupon it was taken over by Geisbauer on loan. Later, it became his property and was substantially expanded by him.

When he came to Covington, he thought that the place looked like the wilderness - there were no homes or people, but only woods. His brewery, located on the corner of Madison and 5th St. stood almost in the midst of the woods. If there were fewer Germans then there are now, then, in my view, they were more united then in social, religious, and political affairs due to their small numbers. Geisbauer was quite a sprightly fellow and was a member for many years of the German Pioneer Society of Covington, but he never sought public office.

List of Pre-1840 Germans in Covington:
Schäffer's directory of Covington for 1839-40 lists the following Germans as residents of Covington:

1. Michael Allgaier (Jaco and Allgaier), owners of a rental stable, 3rd St., between Greenup and Garrard.
2. Bernhard Behle (Bailey), beer brewer;
3. Georg Borel, grocer, on Greenup, between 2nd and 3rd St.
4. Michael Brentle from Bavaria, a laborer
5-6 Adam Engert and his brother, Gustav, from Bavaria, laborers
7. Paul Endress from Bavaria, cooper
8. Jakob Frank, a laborer
9. Peter Gaubert from the Alsace, a plumber
10. Bernhard Gensvittle, a wagoner
11. Jakob Hanhauser from Bavaria, a baker, 2 St., between Greenup and Scott

12. J. G. Hanhauser from Bavaria, a laborer
13. Heinrich Huber (Hoover), a carpenter
14. Peter N. Jonte from France, a brewer
15. Michael Linger from Bavaria, innkeeper, at Greenup, between 2nd and 3rd St.
18. Joseph Lipfrit, a laborer
19. Rudolph Menke, a hotel landlord
20. Jacob Mentz, a worker
21. Friedrich Meyer from the Alsace, a shoemaker
22. Joseph Neuport, a cabinet-maker
23. Georg Niemann from Bavaria, a cooper
24. Alexander Norvaski from Posen, a schoolmaster
25. C. H. Overmann, riverboat man
26. Friederich Perdeszet from Lorraine, an innkeeper
27. Johann Dietrich Pernet from Switzerland, a carpenter
28. Christian Reichert, a laborer
29. Peter Ruckle, a gardener with nursery located one-quarter mile south of Covington
30. Ulrich Schaefter, a laborer
31. Franz Terbacher (Derbacher) from Bavaria, a cabinet-maker
32. Ignatz Warth (Ward)
33. Joseph Weinhage, a cooper
34. Georg Zell, a butcher
35. Wilhelm Zumwalde, a school teacher

To this list, I would add the following members of the German Pioneer Society of Covington, who were not listed in the directory:

36. Georg Bernhard, 1830
37. Heinrich Berte, 1837
38-39 Bernhard Dreesmann and Heinrich Dreesmann, 1839
40. Victor Kaspar Engert, 1834

23

41. Fried. Götz, 1833
43. Clemens Köbbe, 1840
44. Johann Heinrich Meyer, 1838
45. Herman Heinrich Joseph Puthoff, 1839
46. Franz Heinrich Rotert, 1838
47. Wilhelm Willen, 1835

Notes

1. Amos Shinkle (1818-92), the son of German immigrants, was one of the wealthiest and most prominent citizens of Covington. His business in the shipping of coal for which he maintianed a fleet of river boats. As early as 1849, he began investing in real estate, and at the time of his death, he had built close to forty homes. He himself built an extravagant home known as the Castle at 323 E. 2nd St., which the family gave to the Salvation Army in 1914 for use as a hospital; later it built a facility elsewhere and the site is now the location of luxury apartments. At 230-423 E. 2nd St. there is a series of town houses known as Shinkle's Row, a row of renaissance revival townhouses, which was restored in the mid-1920s. See Giglierano, pp. 128-29.

2. See the *Kenton County Court Records*, Vol. I., p. 31.

3. Regarding Wolf, see Heinrich A. Rattermann, "Zwei deutsche Ehrenmänner," *Der Deutsche Pionier*, 10 (1878): 298-308.

4. *Kenton County Court Records*, p. 6.

5. Regarding this outbreak of nativism, see chapter 4.

6. The plat, which Klette laid out, is registered in the *Kenton County Plat Book*, Vol. I, p. 301.

7. Permission was granted for "practicing music on wind instruments and violins." *Kenton County Court Records*, Vol. I, p. 162.

8. Geisbauer purchased the Covington Lager Beer Brewery at 6th and Scott St. from Peter Jonte, who had begun

operation there in 1837. Geisbauer expanded the brewery, and sold it in 1881. It continued operation until 1918. See Robert J. Wimberg, *Cincinnati Breweries*. (Cincinnati: Ohio Book Store, 1989), p. 31.

9. For further information on German-American social life, see Don Heinrich Tolzmann, ed., *German Pioneer Life: A Social History*. (Bowie, Maryland: Heritage Books, Inc., 1992).

10. Regarding the *Mutter Gottes Kirche*, see Paul A. Tenkotte, *A Heritage of Art and Faith: Downtown Covington Churches*. (Covington: Kenton County Historical Society, 1986).

11. *Kenton County Court Records*, Vol. 1, p.30.

12. Charles Nordhoff, *Northern California, Oregon and the Sandwich Islands*. (London: Sampson Low, Marston, Low & Searle, 1874), p. 154.

13. See Carl M. Becker, *The Village: A History of Germantown, Ohio, 1804-1976*. (Germantown, Ohio: Historical Society of Germantown, 1981).

Chapter 3

Accomplishments of the German Pioneers

Occupations and Trades - Heinrich Edler's Wallpaper Printing Company - The Tobacco Factory of the Gedge Brothers - The First Steam-Powered Furniture Factory - Thoss's Beer Garden - Germans in Public Office - Buena Vista - Wilhelm Ernst - German Property Owners - Germans Before 1850 - German Churches and Schools - The First German Church Service and its Preacher, Pastor Ernst - The German Methodist Congregation - Pastors Pichler and Bruner - The German Catholic Church - Father Ferdinand Kühr - The German Protestant Evangelical Church - Pastor Heinrich Dölle - The German Evangelical and Reformed Church - The accomplishments of the German Pioneers of Covington by 1850.

***

The previous chapter should not create the false impression that the Germans of Covington flourished only as inn- and hotel keepers, as they were active in all occupations, which can readily be seen by means of an examination of the list of the German pioneers. Do not our countrymen have the reputation of being the most industrious craftsmen and mechanics?[1]

Early on, Covington did not have all that much in terms of business and industry, but rather served the businessmen of Porkopolis as a suburban place of residence. But gradually, this came to change. At first, few Germans had their own business, and worked in the employ of others, but by the 1870s, Germans had founded and established many

27

businesses in Covington, so that they predominated in the overwhelming majority of trades.[2]

This is due to the fact that in Covington we find the same commercial and enterprising spirit, which is characteristic of Germans. Hence, Heinrich Edler founded in 1842 a wallpaper printing business. As he lacked the necessary capital, and had to borrow the necessary funds, for which he had mortgaged his blocks and printing equipment, the business got off to a bad start, and soon failed. In the same year, the Gedge brothers started a tobacco factory. They were Pennsylvania Germans, and some say they were German immigrants whose name was originally spelled as Götsch. They both spoke fluent German, although their descendants do not.

The plumbing business of Karl Wolf as well as the bakery of Jakob Hahnhauser and Derbacher's furniture cabinet making business have already been mentioned, but we should also mention the first steam-powered furniture factory of Covington, constructed in 1861 by Heinrich Schrötter.

Eduard Thoss pioneered beer gardens in Covington by establishing the Licking Garden in 1843 at the Licking River, in the vicinity of 14th St. This was a popular place well into the 1850s.

Germans, it should be noted, never chased after political office, and aside from the aforementioned justices of the peace, there were relatively few Germans serving in public office in the period before 1850.[3] In this regard, mention should be made that Louis Klette was elected sheriff of Kenton County in 1848. Later, several Germans ran for office, but lost due to the lack of unity for a particular candidate.

Hence, Heinrich Horstmann, one of the most respected citizens of Covington, was defeated a few years ago when he ran for sheriff. And, only a few years ago Bernhard Dreesmann had the same experience for that office. If the Germans would have voted together like the Anglo-Americans do at election time when a German and Anglo-American are on the ballot, then they would have been victorious in both cases, because the Germans of Covington clearly had more votes as a group, although they were not in the majority.

Lower offices have been offered to entice them into the fold of various political parties. Hence, Heinrich Ackermann and Arnold Falkner were elected policemen in 1844, and in 1845 Louis Ries tax collector for the city of Covington. Positions on city council, the school board, and other bodies have been held by Germans ever since. That Joseph Hermes, innkeeper of the German Workers Hall and a member of the German Pioneer Society of Covington, has been a member of the Kentucky state legislature for some time is, of course, a fact well known in the area.

As I mentioned, Heinrich Horstmann was one of the most eminent German pioneers of Covington. In 1846, he founded Buena Vista, now a section of the southern part of Covington, and named it in honor of the place in Mexico, where a battle was won by U.S. General Taylor. Horstmann still resides in Beuna Vista (1877).

Wilhelm Ernst belongs to the German pioneers of Covington, and founded the Northern Bank of Kentucky. He came to Lexington in 1834, and then to Covington in 1838. He hails from Bucks County, Pennsylvania, and his forefathers came from Strassburg in the Alsace. His father was a Presbyterian minister, but could not speak English. His mother was from Dresden, Germany, and died in Covington. Ernst is one of the most well-to-do citizens of Covington, and has extensive property holdings in the area.

German Pioneer Lists

1. Property owners before 1840: Aside from the aforementioned German pioneers, we find the following property owners in the pre-1840 period in Kenton County: Heinrich Ackermann, Joseph Bach, Johann Ballinger, Benjamin F. Bedinger, Bernard Bertlinger, Ernst Busch, Eduard Busch, Hermann Feldhaus, Peter Habig, Samuel Hammel, Clemens Hembrock, Elias Hoffmann, Jakob Hoffmann, Heinrich Horstmann, Mathias Inse, Simon Jäger, Johann Peter Rust, Sebastian Stöhr, Wilhelm Uttenbusch, and Johann Winter; he purchased 1 ½ acres for $87.50 in 1832 at the corner of 4th and Gano St.

2. Property owners from 1840 to 1845: Arnold Benike, Mathias Bürkle (Birkle), Franz Decker (a master stonemason), Joseph Faber, Heinrich Feldhaus, Doris Frey, Heinrich Hammann, Jakob Harding, Lätitia Herbst, Heinrich Huntsmann (died in the flood of 1847/48), Simon Knäbel, Johann Adam Kratzer, Franz Kuntz, Heinrich Kurre, Ferdinand Kühr (for the German Catholic Church), Joseph Kupferle, Bernhard Marschall, Jakob Metz, Ferdinand Möhring, Johann Rothhöfer, Karl Sonntag, Johann Heinrich Welling (died in 1844), B. H. Wellmann, and Wilhelm Wendell.

3. Naturalizations in Kenton County, 1840-44

1. On 21 September 1840: Michael Ufheil (Oaffel) from Baden.

2. On 21 February 1842: Ferdinand Kühr (Kuhr) from Prussia; Heinrich Overmann from Oldenburg.

3. On 20 June 1842: Georg Lauch, probably from Bavaria; Johann Brandlay from Baden.

4. On 17 July 1843: Heinrich Klenke from Hannover; Johann D. Paul from Hannover; Bernhard Hansen from Hannover; Heinrich Venken from Hannover; Dietrich Brons (Bruns) from Hannover; Johann Christian Picot from Hannover; Andreas Jakob from Hannover; Johann Matthis Werking from Hannover; Heinrich Fiber from Hannover; Friedrich Kuhlmann from Hannover; Heinrich Kleinberg from Hannover; Bernhard Gibb from Hannover; Michael Lyons from Hannover; Heinrich Willen from Oldenburg; Johann Heinrich Huntmann from Oldenburg; Johann Wessel Terbe from Oldenburg; Johann Karmann from Oldenburg; Hermann Heinrich Feldhaus from Oldenburg; Johann Kruse from Oldenburg; Franz Decker from Oldenburg; Bernhard Gospole (Gausepohl) from Oldenburg; Karl Gospole from Oldenburg; and Heinrich Kramer from Prussia.

5. On 20 November 1843: Valentin Hagen from Baden.

6. On 20 May 1844: Friedrich Hermann from Saxony.

German churches and congregations were organized later on in Covington as Cincinnati had so many German churches that it first made them unnecessary in Covington.[4] However, gradually the demand for the establishment of German churches and congregations grew due to the rising number of Germans here.

The German Protestants had the first German minister in Covington: the father of Wilhelm Ernst, president of the Northern Bank. He preached in the Pennsylvania German dialect in the Anglo-American Presbyterian church.[5] However, this was not an organized congregation, and his group also was confined to the Pennsylvania Germans here. Presbyterianism moreover did not appeal to the German immigrants, as they held to the teachings of the Lutheran, Evangelical, and Reformed churches, so that the Presbyterians made few inroads with them.[6]

Only the Methodists succeeded at establishing and maintaining a congregation. Their preacher, Heinrich Ernst Pilcher, came to Cincinnati in 1840, and stayed for several years. He received permission from the court in 1840, and stayed for several years. He received permission from the court in 1840 to perform ministerial functions and conduct marriages. The first marriage, hence, then took place on 15 July 1840 between Abraham B. Heimer and Maria Götz. The next German Methodist preacher was Joseph A. Bruner.[7]

The next congregation to be established was that of the German Catholics. In a letter dated 19 November 1844 to the Princely Archdiocesan Administration of the Leopold Foundation of Vienna, the German Catholic patriarch of Covington, Father Ferdinand Kühr, wrote:

"At the time of my arrival in Covington, I found about forty families whose beliefs were to be diverse as to be

32

defined with a single name. I, hence, constructed an alter, which still serves as the high alter in the new church, and made all the necessary arrangements and then held services for several months in a room, which was rented from the Anglo-Americans, where the Rev. Father Salzbacher once celebrated mass. I tried to acquire a building site as quickly as possible, although with borrowed funds. I then began to build and within six months a new brick church, 100' x 50', was ready and was adorned with columns. At the same time, a school was built. I had to be the architect, and acquire all the building materials and supplies, as well as to locate the necessary funds. As the congregation grew from day to day, I soon saw that the church would not be able to hold them all in the near future."[8]

Father Kühr came to America in 1840, and in 1842 arrived in Covington; he passed away on 29 November 1870 after a long and blessed pioneer life.[9]

The room of which he spoke was in the upper floor of the two story house located at the Lower Market, from which the walls had been removed. From this room, the procession to the new church on 6th St. began on 25 March 1843, at which time the cornerstone was laid. The cost of construction was $7,597, and was the first Catholic church in the West. It, of course no longer stands, as on its spot, there now stands the majestic *Mutter Gottes Kirche*, which was erected at a cost of $100,000. Unfortunately, the venerable patriarch was like a second Moses, and was not able to see the church after having led his congregation for almost thirty years. The first church trustees were: Franz Derbacher, Michael Scheinhof, Gerhard Günter, Hermann Feldhaus, and Heinrich Kurre.

The first marriage in the church was between Simon Jakob and Christiana Eisenmann, who were married by Father Kühr on 28 April 1842. The next German Catholic priests to come to Covington were Father Michael Heiss (February 1843) and Father Karl Böswald (January 1844), both of whom came to assist Father Kühr.[10]

Other German Protestant churches followed the founding of the *Mutter Gottes Kirche*. The first preacher who came here from time to time was Pastor Göbel of Cincinnati. This congregation met in the public school, and in 1847 was organized as the German Protestant Evangelical Church with Pastor Heinrich Dölle as its minister. Friedrich Decker, Karl Geisbauer, and others belonged to his church. Pastor Dölle later passed away in Randolph, Indiana.[11]

Notes

1. Regarding the role German-Americans have played in business and industry, see Rudolf Cronau, *German Achievements in America: Rudolf Cronau's Survey History.* Edited by Don Heinrich Tolzmann. (Bowie, Maryland: Heritage Books, Inc., 1995), pp. 108-20.

2. For the Cincinnati historical background for this time period, see Daniel Hurley, *Cincinnati, The Queen City.* (Cincinnati: Cincinnati Historical Society, 1982), pp. 33-62, and Iola Hessler Silberstein, *Cincinnati, Then and Now.* (Cincinnati: The League of Women Voters of the Cincinnati Area, 1982), pp. 25-99.

3. A historical survey of the involvement of German-Americans in politics can be found in Albert B. Faust, *The German Element in the U.S.* (New York: Steuben Society of America, 1927), Vol. 2, pp. 122-200.

4. For a survey of the German-American churches of Cincinnati, see Don Heinrich Tolzmann, *Cincinnati's German Heritage.* (Bowie, Maryland: Heritage Books, Inc., 1994), pp. 52-69.

5. The fact that Ernst preached in the Pennsylvania German dialect reflects the early migration of Pennsylvania Germans to the area.

6. The only history of German-American Presbyterianism is: Clifford H. Fox, *German Presbyterianism in the Upper Mississippi Valley.* (Ypsilanti, Michigan: University Lithographers, 1942).

7. For a history of Methodism, see Paul Douglass, *The Story of German Methodism: Biography of an Immigrant Soul.* (New York: the Methodist Book Concern, 1939).

8. *Berichte der Leopoldinen-Stiftung im Kaiserthume Oesterreich.* 18. Heft (1845): 22ff.

9. For an obituary of Kürr, see *Der Deutsche Pionier.* 2(1870): 319.

10. For a survey of German Catholic history, see Colman James Barry, *The Catholic Church and German-Americans.* (Milwaukee: Bruce, 1953).

11. See "Kurze historische Skizze der Deutschen Vereinigten Evangelischen St. Paulus-Gemeinde in Covington, Ky.," *Der Deutsche Pionier.* 18(1886): 352-53. By 1886, the church had 152 families, a Frauen-Verein of 52 members, a Sunday school of 200 children with 29 teachers, and a choir of 35 members. From 1847 to 1886, there had been 1,830 baptisms; 636 confirmands; 529 weddings; and 776 burials.

Chapter 4

Immigration, Nativism, and the Civil War

The population of Covington grew substantially in the 19th century: 404 in 1824; 2,026 in 1840; 9,408 in 1850; and 16,500 in 1860.[1] From 1820 to 1860 alone, the population expanded eightfold. This tremendous population growth paralleled and reflected the history of immigration, especially the German immigration of that period. German immigration increased after the wars of the Napoleonic era, but greatly picked up after the revolutions of the 1830s and 1848.[2] A cursory examination of the places of origin of the German pioneers in the preceding chapters indicates that the majority were coming from Hannover, Oldenburg, and Bavaria. Smaller numbers were also coming from the Alsace, Baden, Switzerland, and elsewhere. Hence, the German pioneers appeared to primarily be coming from northern Germany.

The influx of waves of immigration in the 19th century was not without problem or friction. These immigrants basically not only altered, but transformed America from a predominantly Anglo Protestant to an increasingly diverse and multi-cultural society. Hence, they shifted the percentages of the populations ingredients, and in so doing met with nativist opposition in the form of the Know-Nothing movement of the 1850s. This reflected an Anglo/immigrant cultural clash on a whole range of issues.[3]

This *Kulturkampf,* or cultural clash, was perhaps best symbolized with Germans in the different conceptions of Sunday. On the one hand, there was the notion of the Puritan Sunday, and on the other, the Continental Sunday, in the perspective of German-Americans. The former held that the Sabbath should be observed with no business and or social activities, whereas the latter held that Sunday afternoons were the time for social functions, festivities and picnics, and that businesses, such as beer gardens, should open for the entire family. Arthur C. Cole explained these differences as follows:

"The tendency toward democratic Sunday amusement gained headway in the towns and cities. This was especially true of the German element which in the summer months repaired to nearby picnic grounds or Sunday gardens and spent the day in merrymaking. To the Germans..., who associated with the Sabbath not only the idea of religious worship but also the festive holiday atmosphere, the gaiety of their Sunday gardens...or the...picnic grounds...seems an inalienable right."

On the same principle, they assumed it was their right to hold parades with their various societies. Cole also notes that the Northwestern Sabbath Convention of 1854 declared that "the vast influx of immigrants joining us from foreign and despotic countries who have learned in their native land to hate the established religion and the Sabbath law as part of it" call "for special prayer and labor in behalf of this portion of the population, to reclaim them from this fatal error."[4]

Obviously, German-American social life was not comprehended here, it was simply a clash of two different lifestyles. Another objection was to the arrival of so many refugees of the failed revolution of 1848, the so-called 48ers. Among them was Karl Heinzen, who came to Louisville, where he edited the *Herold des Westens*, a newspaper. In 1854, he and other 48ers issued the famed Louisville

38

Platform, a German-American position statement on a wide range of social and political issues of the day.[5]

It called for "freedom, wealth, and education" for all, the abolition of slavery, political and social equality for all, endorsed women's rights, called for the minimum wage, the regulation of working hours, and other progressive programs. Although most of them have been enacted and are widely accepted today, they at the time struck the nativists as the hostile critiques of recent arrivals. The Louisville Platform was, hence, viewed as a radical manifesto, and the 48ers were often viewed as radical know-it-all/do-gooders.

Nativists were not only opposed to the liberal elements of the German immigration, but also to the immigration of large waves of Catholics, which appeared to threaten what was viewed as the Anglo Protestant foundations of the country. The opposition to the secular and religious components of the German immigration fused together in the nativism known as the Know-Nothing Movement. This could, and did lead to violence across the country, including the Ohio Valley. In 1855, in Louisville, for example, nativists attempted to keep "foreigners" from voting, thus setting off riots, that killed many. In Cincinnati, in the same year, a nativist mob marched on the Over-the-Rhine district, only to be repelled by gunfire from the German district. According to the *Cincinnati Enquirer* "the Germans fired from all sides and the crowd, which had not expected a determined resistance, fled like rabbits," thus bringing the riots to an abrupt conclusion.[6]

Such feelings of antipathy about the German immigrants, who were also transforming Covington into a city with German-style beer-gardens, a brewery, German churches and societies, were not, therefore, surprising in the 1850s, especially after the founding of a new society, which seemed to typify all the values of the recently arrived 48ers - the Covington Turners.

The first *Turnverein*, or Turner society in America, was founded in Cincinnati under the influence of the popular hero of the revolution in Baden, Germany, Friedrich Hecker. He came to Cincinnati in 1848, and was enthusiastically received by Cincinnati Germans, who were sympathetic to the cause of the 48ers. On 22 October 1848, Hecker arrived in Cincinnati and was jubilantly greeted by a torchlight parade, and on the following day, several German immigrants, many of whom had been Turners in Germany, discussed the founding of a Turner society in Cincinnati,[7]

The word Turner came from the German word "turnen," which meant to turn, move, and exercise, as the Turners believed in the "cultivation of rational training, both intellectual and physical, in order that the members may become energetic, patriotic citizens of the Republic, who could and would represent and protect common human liberty by word and deed."[8] Hence, the Turners were not only a gymnastic organization, but also were active in the social, cultural, and political realms.

To realize their goals, they held gymnastic exercises, sponsored musical sections, while intellectual gymnastics were furthered by libraries, theaters, lectures, etc.   On Sundays, hiking tours were organized, and to circumvent Sunday liquor laws, a bar was usually set up in the club house.

With this kind of organization new on the scene in Covington, it was not long before it became the target of local nativists. This nativist outburst against the Turners is well described by Emil Klauprecht's German-American history:

"On Pentecost Monday of the following year (1856) there were numerous confrontations between the Turners and the mobs in Covington. During their picnic on the field beneath Whitehall, the Turners were constantly plagued by a group of youths from 10 to 14 years old, who had followed them from Covington. Constantly offering insults, they (the youths) threw sticks and stones and finally, one of them ripped a glass of beer out of the hand of one of the Turners. The affected Turner hit the boy in the mouth, whereupon the boy pulled a pistol and the spectacle began. The boy ran to Covington and spread the rumor that the Turners meant to murder 9 to 10 young Covington boys,. Naturally the Turners remained ignorant of the resultant excitement. Between 5 and 6, with music playing and the Stars and Stripes waving, they began their way home.

Near Whitehall, bands of young people had gathered and began to attack the Turners with stones. As they came closer to Covington, one man stepped up, laid a hand on one of the Turners, and attempted to pull him out of the ranks. The Turner resisted and his companions came to his assistance. The man (who stepped out) was Marshal Butts of Covington. The Turner did not recognize the man of his office.

The procession continued; the crowd following with growing excitement. The marshal stayed close to his man and several times tried to apprehend him. Finally general fighting broke out, stones flew from both sides and pistols were fired.

Marshal Butts' arm was shattered, and Deputy Sheriff Harvey was seriously wounded in the arm. The Turners marched through Covington, followed on both sides by an agitated crowd. They crossed the Licking bridges and passed through Newport, making the ferry landing, where they intended to cross over.

During this time, the Covington fire bells were ringing, which further increased the crowd. The Turners formed up in rows and columns on the east side of the landing, with their front facing west. The crowd stayed below York St., from where they began throwing stones at the Turners. In response to the attack, the Turners fired several shots in return. The shots increased the overall anger of the crowd, most of whom were from Covington. Many of these individuals appeared to be almost insane, calling on 'Old Kentuck' to destroy 'the Dutchmen'. Several rushed to the garrison and demanded assistance from the troops. Mayor Fearons later repeated that request; however the officers refused to participate in the fight without authorization from Washington.

The Turners straightened up their rows. In their gray linen jackets and caps topped with greenery, they posed a striking contrast to the mob. Several had muskets armed with bayonets. They stood peacefully and quietly, strictly obeying the orders of their officers. Sheriff Stricker and Police Officer Miller earnestly tried to calm the mob and forestall a bloody fight. The Turners remained quiet and made no difficulty. At this point, the mayors of Covington and Newport arrived on the scene. The former, Mr. Foley, immediately demanded that the Turners surrender their weapons and place themselves at the disposition of the civil authorities. The mob supported this demand and indicated that it would not be appeased if the weapons were not surrendered.

At that moment, the ferryboat 'Bee' of Captain Air's Line approached the shore with a huge number of passengers from Cincinnati on board. Mayor Fearsons would not let the boat land there. The passengers were disembarked onto a float, opposite the garrison. In response to the demand to surrender their weapons, Captain Müller, the Turner Commander, stated that his men would not hesitate to comply, if they could do so in safety; however, since that was not possible due to the presence of the hostile crowd, they would have to retain their weapons for self-protection. The police, however, would encounter no opposition in arresting those persons guilty of breaking the law.

The police moved through the ranks without encountering any opposition and arrested four Turners. This did not appease the crowd, which demanded that the Turners lay down their arms. The officials again repeated this demand. The captain respectfully declined, but at the same time ordered the bayonets to be dismounted and sheathed.

That was a critical moment. The officials were powerless, the Turners quiet and determined, the crowd aroused to a frenzy. 'Go and finish'em! Where are you, Kentucky Fellows?' screamed several voices. Finally, the Turners decided to seek refuge in the Turner Hall. Several stones flew against them; but not a word, not a curse came from the ranks of the Turners. They went up York St. Across from the courthouse and again at the corner of Orchard St. came the demand to the group in the name of the mayor to give up their weapons. The answer could be read in the faces of the Turners, who, to the astonishment of all who were following the events, reached their Hall with everyone of their men without a wound.

Again, Mayor Foley demanded that the Turners surrender their weapons. However, Judge Stallo replied that, since he (the mayor) could not defend the Turners against the mob, the Turners guaranteed that no one would leave the Hall and they would surrender the following morning to the authorities for disposition. Sheriff Stricker needlessly surrounded the Hall with a cordon of Kentuckians, to prevent anyone from escaping. The crowd slowly dispersed.

After a long debate, it was decided that all of the prisoners would be given over to Kenton county authorities. After deliberating for 7 days, the preliminary hearing, conducted by two Justices of the Peace, recommended to the Kenton County court in Covington that felony charges be brought against 31 Turners. Each one had to post $2,000 bond, to ensure appearance before the court. The entire $62,000 was immediately put up in Newport, Kentucky by two honored Germans, Daniel Wolf and Peter Constanz.

The trial dragged through several sessions of the county court and ended with an acquittal for every defendant, whose defense was conducted in a masterly fashion by Judge Stallo."[9]

The 1856 nativist clash of the nativists with the Turners was the major such outbreak of hostility in Covington before the Civil War. Here as elsewhere, nativist hostilities began to subside in the latter years of the 1850s in the face of the rising sectional crisis, which culminated in the Civil War. The rise of the Republican Party, and the huge influx of German-Americans into the party of Lincoln, further contributed to their political correctness and acceptance in American society. Their status was further enhanced by their enthusiastic support for the Union cause, resulting in the formation of all-German regiments in nearby Cincinnati and Indiana, in which many Covington Germans no doubt served.[10]

Although nativism had subsided with the advent of the Civil War, Covington was a different place than it had been two decades earlier: its population had increased eightfold, and waves of German immigrants had landed on the southern side of the Ohio River, and the foundations of Covington's German element had been firmly established.

45

Notes

1. Giglierano, *Cincinnati*, p. 123.

2. Regarding the German immigrations, see Willi Paul Adams, *The German-Americans: An Ethnic Experience.* Translated and Adapted by Lavern J. Rippley and Eberhard Reichmann. (Indianapolis: Max Kade German-American Center, Indiana University-Purdue University at Indianapolis, 1993), pp. 2-11

3. For a survey of the history of nativism, see Ray Allen Billington, *The Protestant Crusade, 1800-1860: A Study of the Origins of American Nativism.* (Chicago: Quadrangle Books, 1964). For studies of nativism in the Greater Cincinnati area, see William A. Baughin, "Nativism in Cincinnati Before 1860," (M.A. Thesis, University of Cincinnati, 1963) and Agnes G. McGann, "Nativism in Kentucky in 1860," (M.A. Thesis, Catholic University of America, 1944).

4. Cole as cited in A. E. Zucker, *The Forty-Eighters: Political Refugees of the German Revolution of 1848.* (New York: Columbia University Pr., 19509), p. 93.

5. For further information on the 48ers, see Don Heinrich Tolzmann, ed., *The German-American Forty-Eighters, 1848-1998.* (Indianapolis: Max Kade German-American Center & Indiana German Heritage Society, 1998).

6. Cited in Owen Findsen, "Riots Disrupted But Couldn't Sway Election," *Cincinnati Enquirer.* (10 March 1996).

7. See Don Heinrich Tolzmann, "150th Anniversary - The Cincinnati Central Turners," *Society for German-American Studies Newsletter.* 18:3(1997) 18-19.

46

8. Zucker, *The Forty-Eighters*, p.93.

9. Klauprecht, *The German Chronicle,* p. 194-95. Stallo (1823-1900), was a widely respected German-American judge in Cincinnati. For a collection of his writing, which include coverage of the topic of nativism, see J. B. Stallo, *Reden, Abhandlungen und Briefe.* (New York: E. Steiger, 1893).

10. Regarding German-Americans in the Civil War, see Tolzmann, *The German-American Soldier*, pp. 194-95.

Chapter 5

The German Pioneer Society of Covington

In 1869, the German Pioneer Society of Cincinnati
was formed for the purpose of preserving the German heritage
by recording and documenting German-American history for
future generations. It accomplished this goal through its
meetings, programs, festivities, but particularly by means of
its outstanding historical journal, *Der Deutsche Pionier*,
edited by Heinrich A. Rattermann. This contained articles,
essays, reviews, bibliographies, as well as news and reports
from the Society and affiliated Pioneer Societies.[1]

Among its affiliates was the German Pioneer Society
of Covington, established in 1877. In the year it was founded,
Rattermann had presented three lectures for the Society in
Covington dealing with Covington's German heritage, which
were subsequently published in the Society's journal. The
founding of the Society clearly reflected an interest on the part
of the Covington Germans in recording and preserving their
history.[2]

In 1878, Rattermann again spoke in Covington on the
occasion of the first anniversary of the German Pioneer
Society of Covington, asking the Pioneers: "Can any other
nation hold up great such great characters as the Germans?
What nation has greater poets and writers, greater musicians,
greater artists, greater mechanics, more learned people and
philosophers, greater military leaders and statesman, in all
greater people to be proud of than the German
nation?...Therefore, let us be proud and many will respect us
and not call us 'Dutch' any more. Let us not be ashamed to

be called German and soon they will stop calling us Dutchmen."

He also noted that the efforts of the German Pioneer societies "are going in that direction. They are working to raise the spirit of self among its members and to make known the history and the cultural development of the Germans in this country. The Germans have already made history in this country in spite of the fact that they try to keep it a secret. Already in this country the Germans have shown their knowledge in every branch...Indeed, we can be proud of the accomplishments of the Germans in this country. To increase the German pride and self-esteem and to encourage our descendants to aspire for higher things, is the purpose and task of the German Pioneer societies; it is a mission in which they should be active. Let us pursue this direction and you and your children will reap its blessing."[3]

Rattermann, hence, was explaining that German-Americans had a history and heritage of which they could be proud, and that it should be recorded for the future generations, and that this was the goal of the German Pioneer Society. Therefore, by the 1870s, the Covington Germans had arrived at the stage where they were becoming concerned and interested in their historical identity as German-Americans. They recognized they now had a history, a German-American history, and one worthy of recording.

In 1902, on the occasion of the 25th anniversary of the German Pioneer Society of Covington, the history of the organization was published, and provides further insight into the Covington Germans.[4] It reads as follows:

"The word "Pioneer" explains in itself the goals and motives of a society of seasoned men, who, to a certain extent, provide the foundations of a strong community. During the twenty-five years of its existence, the Pioneer Society of Covington has carried out beneficial work within the community both directly and indirectly, and through the unselfish efforts of its members the German city of Covington has remained German, industrious, and, from a moral perspective, far superior to many other cities. This the German Pioneer has accomplished, who through his example, his knowledge, and his resolution has pointed the younger generation in the right direction. The Pioneer of today has a history behind him full of deprivations. His hair has become gray in the struggle for survival. His hands bear witness to the hard labor by which he provided for himself and his loved ones. Some of these Pioneers have been blessed by the goods of earthly success, which they have attained through their honest labor; to others, fortune has not been particularly kind, despite their efforts throughout a long and upright life. But all are happy and satisfied and look forward to a joyful evening of life, which they have earned honestly.

In the following we will provide a short overview of the activity of the Pioneer Society:

In the month of April in the year 1877 nineteen German citizens of Covington had the intention of joining the Pioneer Society in our neighboring city of Cincinnati, in order to become members of such a club temporarily. The Cincinnati Pioneer Mr. H. Rattermann, well known in all circles, encouraged the gentlemen to form an affiliated club in Covington itself, however. Thereupon the gentlemen in question undertook the initial steps and through the German press requested all German immigrants who were over forty years of age and who had resided for twenty years in the country to assemble on May 6 of that year at 8:00 o'clock in the evening in the Workers' Hall in order to found a German Pioneer Society. Many responded to this invitation, and the first assembly was a very enthusiastic one. Mr. Joseph Hermes was chosen as provisional President and Mr. Gerhard Heinrich Schleutker as provisional secretary. It was also decided to organize the newly formed Pioneer Society on the same principles as that of Cincinnati. Moreover, a committee was set up to work out a constitution. The committee consisted of Mssrs. Georg Welling, Moritz Blaier and Conrad Deisler. How much the Germans longed for the organization of such a club was shown by the delightful circumstances that ninety gentlemen inscribed themselves as members immediately. The first officers were the following gentlemen:

President--Georg Welling
Vice-President..Henry Deglow
Secretary--B. H. F. Hellebusch
Treasurer--Henry Adams
Governing Board--Conrad Deisler,
   John Herold, G. H. Schleutker,
   Victor Engert, B. Marschall

Welling's Hall was established as a regular meeting place and renamed the Pioneer Hall. The German tradition had received with the formation of this society a solid basis, and the German idea of community took firm root, so that nothing further stood in the way of the growth, blossoming, and prospering of the Pioneer Society.

On August 3 of this year the Pioneers decided to accept the invitation of the Cincinnati Pioneer Society and to take part as a body in the celebration of the ninth anniversary of their founding. Ninety-three members participated. In the same meeting it was decided to hold the first Fall Celebration in Ruder's Garden (currently Eichler's Garden), in which the tidy sum of $83.00 was raised.

The lack of a flag was discussed at the first meeting of the year 1878, and a committee of seven members was formed to discuss a remedy for the situation. The committee contacted a Ladies Committee immediately, which consisted of Mrs. Catherina Bunning, Mrs. Wm. Menninger, Mrs. Adam Geiswein, Mrs. Conrad Deisler, Mrs. H. W. Schleutker, Mrs. Georg Welling, Mrs. Conrad Ackermann and Mrs. G. H. Deglow.

On February 25, 1878, the first celebration of the birthday of the Father of the Fatherland, George Washington, was held, in which Mr. and Mrs. Adam Geiswein represented George and Martha Washington. As German joviality and humor began to produce their effects in the course of the birthday celebration, the Pioneers received a not inconsiderable surprise when the Ladies Committee presented them with their gift of a flag of the United States. Mrs. Catherina Bunning, surrounded by eight young ladies in costume, made the presentation. The president, Mr. Georg Welling, thanked the noble and high-minded ladies in the name of the society and paid them the tribute their work and efforts deserved. Mr. H. Rattermann gave the keynote address and proceeded to dedicate the flag. Dr. Uberdick held an uplifting speech in English, which made a deep impression on the Pioneers.

In the same year the memorial fund was begun, and the first Pioneer to depart this mortal life was F. H. Meyer; he died on July 30, 1878, at the age of fifty-two. The second in the same year was Henry Berti, the third Carl Geisbauer, the Pioneer brewer, who died on August 19, 1878, and whose brewery was taken over and significantly enlarged by John Brenner in 1868.

In 1886 Welling's Hall could no longer accommodate the Pioneers, and they sought and found a new home in Jos. Geiser's hall on the corner of Pike and Washington Streets. The first meeting was held here on March 4 of the same year, in the course of which it was decided to put on, for the sake of variety, a large-scale celebration. It was to be a steamer excursion to Ripley, Ohio, where there was also a Pioneer Society, to which the old gentlemen intended to pay a fraternal visit. On the day of the outing, June 24, 1886, they were received by the Ripley Pioneer Society in the most hospitable and comradely fashion.

In 1888 the Pioneers decided to set the age of admission for prospective members at sixty-five; later they saw themselves obliged to reduce it significantly, however, in order to maintain the number of members at the previous level. An important suggestion, for the period by no means impossible, was made by Mr. Ferdinand Nienaber on July 7 of the same year on the occasion of his conclusion of his duties as president. He advanced the idea that the Pioneers as an organization were strong enough to build their own home, where they could hold their meetings and social events. Unfortunately, the suggestion did not find favor in the eyes of the other Pioneers, and the matter was not mentioned again.

The Pioneers had hardly conducted their business in Geiser's Hall for four years when one faction began to call for the relocation of the Society's meeting place. As a result, the Pioneer Society returned on April 3, 1890, to its "first love,"

Stängle's Hall (formerly Welling's Pioneer Hall), and settled in there.

The question of a flag was again a subject of much discussion among the members in 1893. They wanted very much to have a pretty club flag. It was not only the problematic nature of the matter, but also many other circumstances that led to the postponement of this wish.

In 1896 the Pioneers had again become dissatisfied with their hall, for which reason they moved to the Central Garden, where they still have their main meeting place and where they are celebrating the twenty-fifth anniversary.

After twenty-three years, on June 7, 1900, a committee was charged with the task of finding the means for procuring a club flag. It consisted of the Pioneers G. Wieschörster, F. Schummer, and Adam Geiswein. Naturally it was again the women "weaving heavenly roses into earthly life," as the saying goes, who rose to the occasion and immediately went into action to secure the appropriate banner. The following ladies were involved: Ms. Wm. Riedlin, Ms. A. Geiswein, Ms. Friedrich Brenner, Ms. H. H. Riehemann, Ms. B. Staggenborg, Ms. C. Schlitzberger, Ms. Jos. Schummer, Ms. G. H. Wieschörster, and Ms. Hermann Brinkmann. The flower of womanhood got to work immediately, so that the magnificent flag was ready to be presented on September 9, 1900, the day of the twenty-third anniversary of the founding of the society.

The administrative council was charged with arrangements for the celebration, which took place in Saalfeld's Garden in Milldale. Ms. Wm. Riedlin made the presentation and gave the splendid double flag to the president of the Pioneer Society, Mr. Wm. Riedlin. Mr. Riedlin thanked the ladies most cordially in the name of the society for their unselfish effort and held a speech to participants in the celebration that explained in detail the noble purpose of dedicating the flag. The momentous celebration proceeded in an extremely harmonious fashion, making an unforgettable impression on all participants and giving the Pioneer Society an even firmer hold that cannot be shaken. (Translator's note: A list of the founding Pioneers with the dates of their birth indicated by "geb." and date of their immigration indicated by "ausgewandert" follows, beginning on the sixth page of this history and ending on the ninth page. Those individuals whose names are marked by an asterisk were still alive in 1902.)

On December 2, 1897, the efforts of the Pioneer Society led to the founding of a Society of the Sons of the Pioneers, which remained in existence for a while. Had the members shown the same German spirit and German solidarity as did their fathers, it would still be flourishing today.

One of the most dedicated treasurers of the German Pioneer society was the pioneer Felix Fritz, who was elected no fewer than thirteen times to this office of responsibility, which he carried out in such an admirable manner that the Pioneer Society presented him with a golden Pioneer Badge as a sign of their esteem. He occupied the office until his death.

The names of the presidents of the Pioneer Society since its founding follows: (Translator's note" This list is included on the tenth page of this history.)

Pioneer Fritz Stängle occupied the office of secretary eight years to the utmost satisfaction of the society. His dates of office extended from 1889 through 1896.

Mr. Henry Linnemann, one of the oldest Pioneers, came to this region in 1850 and joined the local club in 1882.

On the day of its anniversary the society has a membership of two hundred and thirty-two.

In the twenty-five years of the society's existence, one hundred and thirty-four members have departed this mortal life.

The current officers of the Pioneer Society are as follows:

President--Wilhelm Riedlin
Vice President--George Harmeling
First Secretary Carl Schlitzberger
Second Secretary--H.H. Albers
Treasurer--Jos. Wehrmann
Collector--F. H. Wieschörster
Flag Bearer-Adam Kraft
Administrative Council--August Grote, Heinrich Schmidt, Conrad Schmidt, Lambert Determann and Moritz Eichler

It is a beautiful, noble, and sublime custom of the German Pioneers to celebrate each year the birthday of the Father of the Fatherland, the great George Washington, who was "first in peace and first in war and first in the hearts of his countrymen." The German Pioneers celebrate him, therefore, as the first and most outstanding pioneer of freedom and independence, as an ideal in terms of intelligence, resolution, and bravery, both in the field and in council. German hearts are drawn to the great pioneer George Washington for another reason, too: his love of Germans. His was familiar with their loyalty and reliability, and he respected in them those qualities that he himself possessed. His bodyguard consisted exclusively of Germans. He knew that he could count on them. The tribute that the German Pioneers pay him each year is therefore appropriate.

One of the most desirable aspects of the Pioneer Society is incontestably the relaxed conversation that takes place after every meeting. The members exchange blessed memories of times long past, and serious and humorous anecdotes alternate in colorful procession. Through this fine custom the members look into each others' hearts, and as a consequence, a single bond of friendship unites them. The successes of the society are due not least of all to Pioneer William Riedlin, the popular perennial president, who is able to bring joy quickly to even the saddest face whenever he appears. He is held in the highest esteem by all members on account of his upstanding and honest German character, of which the Pioneers can rightly be proud. (Translator's note: The following description of Dr. Blau accompanies his picture.)

Dr. Blau was one of the most respected and popular founders of the society and a physician of eminent capabilities. He was born on May 18, 1832, in Veringendorf in Hohenzollern-Sigmaringen and began his career in Graz and Vienna. He completed his doctorate in the university of the latter city. Thereupon he immigrated to the United States on the ship "Premier," on which he held the position of ship's doctor. He settled on August 2, 1857, in Covington and soon became a sought-after doctor. He died on April 3, 1902, after years of service to humanity, mourned by his family and his many friends and fellow citizens. In him one of those noble Germans went to his eternal reward for whom honesty and loyalty were the main virtue. Let his memory be honored. His son, Dr. F. M. Blau, also a sought-after physician, will exercise the difficult profession of his father in the same way."

Notes

1. For further information on Rattermann and *Der Deutsche Pionier*, see Don Heinrich Tolzmann, *German American Literature*. (Metuchen, New Jersey: Scarecrow Pr., 1977), pp. 240-44.

2. A collection of the records of the German Pioneer Society of Covington can be found at the Kenton County Public Library, *German Pioneer Society of Covington, Kentucky, 1877-1902*. (Covington: Kenton County Public Library, 1988).

3. See *German Pioneer Society of Covington*, n.p.

4. The 25th anniversary history of the society was translated by Thomas H. Leech, Northern Kentucky University. Its original title in German was: *Gedenkblatt zum 25-jaehrigen Jubilaeum des Deutschen Pionier-Vereins von Covington, Ky., gehalten am Montag, 9 Juni 1902.* (Covington, Ky.: Standard Printing Works, 1902).

Chapter 6

The German-American Alliance

The Covington Turners and the German Pioneer
Society were two of the oldest and major German societies in
Covington, but certainly not the only ones. By the early
1900s, there were 27 organizations affiliated with the
German-American Alliance of Covington, the umbrella
organization for the German societies of the area. The
Covington Alliance was affiliated with the German-American
State Alliance of Kentucky, which in turn was affiliated with
the National German-American Alliance, which was
headquartered in Philadelphia.

The National Alliance was formed in Philadelphia on
German-American Day, the 6th of October 1901. Its platform
and early history, as recorded by Rudolf Cronau, provide a
blueprint to the philosophy of the Alliance and its state and
city branches, such as the Kentucky Alliance and the
Covington Alliance, and reads as follows:

Principles of the National German American Alliance
of the United States of America

The National German American Alliance aims to
awaken and strengthen the sense of unity among the people of
German origin in America with a view to promote useful and
healthy development of the power inherent in them as a
united body for the mutual energetic protection of such
legitimate desires and interests not inconsistent with the
common good of the country and the rights and duties of
good citizens; to check nativistic encroachments; to maintain

60

and safeguard the good friendly relations existing between America and the old German fatherland. To read the history of German immigration is to be convinced how much it has contributed to the advancement of the spiritual and economic development of this country, and to realize what it is still destined to contribute, and how the German immigrant has at all times stood by his adopted country in weal or in woe.

The Alliance demands therefore the full honest recognition of these merits and opposes every attempt to belittle them. Always true to the adopted country, ever ready to risk all for its welfare, sincere and unselfish in the exercise of the duties of citizenship, respecting the law -- still remains the watch-word! It has no exclusive interests in view, nor the founding of a State within a State, but sees in the centralization of the inhabitants of German origin the shortest road and the surest guarantee for the attainment of the aims set forth in this constitution. It calls therefore on all German organizations -- as the organized representatives of the German spirit and manners -- to co-operate with it for their development, and recommends further the formation of Societies in all the states of the Union for the preservation of the interest of German Americans, looking toward an eventual centralization of these societies into a great German American Alliance, and would have all German societies consider it a duty and an honor to join the organization in their respective States. The Alliance engages to labor firmly and at all times with all legal means at its command for the maintenance and propagation of its principles, and to defend them energetically wherever and whenever they are in danger. Its purposes are the following platform:

1. The Alliance, as such, refrains from all interference in party politics reserving, however, the right and duty to defend its principles also in the political field, in case these should be attacked or endangered by political measures. The Alliance will inaugurate and support all legislation for the common good that is sure to find unanimous approval of its members.

2. Questions and matters of religion are strictly excluded.

3. It recommends the introduction of the study of German into the public schools on the following broad basis:

Along with English, German is a world language; wherever the pioneers of civilization, trade and commerce have penetrated, we find the people of both languages represented; wherever, real knowledge of another language prevails more generally, there an independent, clear and unprejudiced understanding is more easily formed and mutual friendly relations promoted.

4. We live in an age of progress and invention; the pace of our time is rapid, and the demands on the individual are inexorable; the physical exertion involved increases the demand on the bodily force; a healthy mind should live in a healthy body. For these reasons the alliance will labor for the introduction of systematic and practical gymnastic (physical culture) instruction in the public schools.

5. It further declares in favor of taking the school out of politics, for only a system of education that is free from

political influence can offer the people real and satisfactory schools.

6. It calls on all Germans to acquire the right of citizenship as soon as they are legally entitled to it, to take an active part in public life, and to exercise their right at the polls fearlessly and according to their own judgement.

7. It recommends either a liberal and modern interpretation or the abolition of laws, that put unnecessary difficulties in the way of acquiring the right of citizenship, and frequently entirely prevent it.

8. It opposes any and every restriction of immigration of healthy persons from Europe, exclusive of convicted criminals and anarchists.

9. It favors the abolition of antiquated laws no longer in accordance with the spirit of the times, which check free intercourse and restrict the personal freedom of the citizen, and recommends a sane regulation of the liquor traffic in conformity with good common-sense and high ethical principles.

10. It recommends the founding of educational societies which will foster the German language and literature, teach those anxious to learn, and arrange courses of lectures on art and science and questions of general interest.

11. It recommends a systematic investigation of the share Germans have had in the development of their adopted country, in war and in peace, in all kinds of German

American activity, from the earliest days, as the basis for the founding and continuance of a German-American history.

12. The Alliance advocates all legal and economically correct measures for the protection of the forests of the United States.

13. We deem it our duty to assist as much as possible original ideas and inventions of Americans of German birth or descent for the common good of our country.

14. It reserves the right to extend or supplement this platform when new conditions within the scope of its time and aims make it desirable or necessary.

This platform contains nothing whatever that is not in full accord with good citizenship and to the best interests of the whole country. In recognition of this fact the Alliance was, after a very painstaking investigation of its aims and purposes incorporated on February 27, 1907, by an Act of Congress.

The Alliance was fortunate enough to find in Dr. Charles John Hexamer an enthusiastic leader, who since the founding of the organization has kept it in the right channel. That the movement met the enthusiastic response from the whole German American population, is seen by the rapid extension of the Alliance, which now has organizations in every State of the Union, even in Hawaii.

Its whole membership amounts to about 2½ to 3 millions. the national conventions are held biannually and have taken place as follows: 1903 at Baltimore; 1905 at Indianapolis; 1907 at New York; 1909 at Cincinnati; 1911 at Washington; 1913 at St. Louis; and 1915 at San Francisco.

One of the first acts of the constitution convention of October 6, 1901, was the adoption of a motion made by Rudolf Cronau, the delegate from New York, that a monument be erected to the memory of Franz Daniel Pastorius and the Founders of Germantown. For this purpose the Alliance collected from its members $30,000, to which the U. S. Congress in recognition of the great contributions of the German element to American culture granted an additional sum of $25,000. the monument executed by Albert Jaegers in New York, has been described in another chapter.

In like manner the memory of the Major-Generals von Steuben and Mühlenberg has been honored by the erection of beautiful statues in Washington, D.C., in the Valley Forge National Park, in Utica, N.Y., and in Philadelphia. The Johnstown branch of the Pennsylvania Organization erected a monumental fountain with the bust of Joseph Schantz, the first settler of that city, a German. The United Societies of New York City did homage to the memory of Jakob Leisler by planting an oak tree in City Hall Park. In response to its advocacy the name of a public park bordering on East River was changed to Carl Schurz Park. The New York State organization succeeded in having a bill passed in legislature by which the old homestead of Nicolas Herchheimer was purchased and made a historic museum, containing relics on the General and the war for independence. To Major-General

65

Peter Osterhaus and to the widow of Franz Sigel pensions were secured. Large sums were collected and distributed to the San Francisco Earthquake Sufferers and to the wounded, and the war-widows and orphans in Germany and Austro-Hungary. The sums raised for these humanitarian purposes amount to many hundreds of thousands of dollars.

In accordance with its principles the German American Alliance promotes the culture of gymnastics, song, music, art and the study of German language and literature in public schools. By pointing out the great achievements of the German element in America it seeks to secure a proper respect and fair regard for this element. By founding a Junior Order in 1908 it seeks to inspire the younger generation to continue in the works of their fathers, and to endeavor the same industriousness, enterprise and patriotism. By lifting its members from the narrow limits of club-life, it induces them to participate as true citizens of the Republic in all public affairs. Through its committees it makes practical recommendations for the preservation and wise utilization of all natural resources of our country.

And so it strives in many directions to win recognition for its motto:" "Always true to our adopted country; ever ready to risk all for its welfare; sincere and unselfish in the duties of citizenship; respecting the law -- is and always shall remain the watchword."[1]

The platform and early history of the Alliance provides some basic insight into where the Alliance stood on a whole range of issues, and also illuminated the importance of the German heritage, as well as the values considered important by German-Americans. In 1909, the National

66

Alliance held its national convention in Cincinnati, at which time the state branches reported on affairs in their respective states. The State Alliance of Kentucky reported on its history, indicating that the first Alliance had been formed in Louisville in 1906 followed by one in Newport, and that the first state convention was held in 1907, and a second one in Newport, which included representatives from Louisville, Newport, Covington, and Bernstadt. Hence, the German-American Alliance of Covington was formed in 1906/07.

On 11 July 1909, the third annual state convention of the Kentucky Alliance was held in Covington at the Turner Hall, and the following principles adopted: First, members should only vote for those candidates, who were in accord with the platform of the National German-American Alliance. Second, the Kentucky Alliance strongly embraced "personal liberty" and opposed any attempt to limit individual freedom as guaranteed by the U.S. Constitution. third, the Alliance pledged to work for the introduction of German instruction in the public schools and to encourage the state legislature to endorse physical education in the schools. Fourth, it stated its opposition to prohibition, claiming that it would cause a great financial loss to the state, which would amount to one-third of the tax base of Kentucky, not to mention the taxes on the buildings and workers involved in the trade, as well as the thousands of people who would be thrown out of work if prohibition be enacted. Finally, the State Alliance pledged to do its utmost to oppose any and all attempts at establishing prohibition in Kentucky.

The State Alliance meeting in Covington also reported that it had turned in petitions against prohibition to the state conventions of the Democratic and Republican parties of the state. As a follow-up to these statements, parades were held

67

in the fall across the state against prohibition. Moreover, in August 1908, a Civil Liberties League was formed to work further on the prohibition issue. the Alliance took pride that prohibition candidates had been defeated in recent elections and that its work had not been in vain. State president John Hubig closed by admonishing Kentucky's German-Americans to "keep your eyes open, there are still hard battles ahead, as our opponents are very active."[2]

The Covington Alliance had its headquarters at the office of Wolff Printing Co., 404 Scott St., as its owner Alban Wolff served as Secretary of the Covington Alliance. Wolff, who printed an extensive amount of materials in German and English for German-American societies and churches in the entire Greater Cincinnati area, played a prominent role in German-American affairs of the region.[3] Indeed, his company would continue German-English printing into the 1980s. The following were the societies and their delegates to the German-American Alliance of Covington:

1. Deutsche Schuetzen Gesellschaft (German Sharpshooters Society) - Frank A. Averbeck, John P. Heidel, Nic Brake.

2. Deutscher Pionerverein (German Pioneer Society) - George Harmeling, H. H. Albers, Joseph Hermes, Conrad Klumppe, Joseph Welp.

3. Covington Turngemeinde (Covington Turners) - Mr. Riedlin, Alban Wolff, George Schneider.

4. Badischer Unterstuetzungs-Verein (Badensian Mutual Aid Society) - Henry Binz, Frank Hauser.

/

5.   Lewisburg   Schuetzen-Gesellschaft   (Lewisburg Sharpshooters Society) - H. A. Perny, George F. Roth, Carl Behle.

6. Arbeiter-Verein (German Workers Society) - Adolph Ante, August Stark, Wm. Kranz.

7.   Turner-Maennerchor (Turners' Men's Choir) - Ernst Ulrich, Julius H. Ehrlenbach, Chas. Pfetzer.

8.   Deutscher Landwehrverein (German Home Guard Society) - John Brecht, Louis Schuerrer.

9.   Deutscher Maenner-Unterstuetzungsverein (German Men's Mutual Aid Society) - Jos. Deutenberg, Jr., Carl Ruehmeier, Jos. Damal.

10. Advance Mutual Aid Society - Ben Sanning, J. C. Geiger, Charles Saalfeld.

11. Unique Mutual Aid Society - Peter P. Thiel, Chas. A. Vonderschmitt, John Unlage.

12. Golden Eage Mutual Aid Society - Fred Wachs, Wm. Stadlaender, John Sanning.

13. Standard Mutual Aid Society - Al Rammler, Henry Tumler, Chas. Sehlhorst.

14. Magnolia Mutual Aid Society - Paul Bechtold, Geo. Brill, Adolph Forbriger.

15. Summer Mutual Aid Society - Edward Memmering, Barney Berns, William Hanekamp.

16. Wizard Outing Club - Herman Berling, Julius Schulte, Chas. Dietz.

17. Linden Mutual Aid Society - Ernst Wachs, John Reitz, Chas. Fischer.

18. Bavarian Benevolent Society - Henry Gastinger, Charles Koenig, Henry Wendt.

19. Crescent Avenue Smokers Casino - Otto Knupfer, Fred Freund, Joseph Cappel.

20. Central Mutual Aid Society - Frank Staggenborg, John Schulte, John Kasing.

21. Fidelity Mutual Aid Society - Andy Maier, W. Funke, Fred Frilling.

22. American Mutual Aid Society - Andy Maier, W. Funke, Fred Frilling.

23. Anchor Social Club - J. Luebbers.

24. Progressive Mutual Aid - B. H. Bockweg, Wm. Strattmann, John Dierkes.

25. Sunny Side Mutual Aid - Henry Gruenloh, Frank Koester, John Merose.

26. First Ward M. P.A. - Jos. L. Ruh, Jos. Berling, Ernst Hegge.

27. West End Deutscher Maenner-Unterstuetzungs-Verein (West End German Men's Mutual Aid Society) - Gottlieb Asimus, John C. Hoerstling, John E. Saalfeld.

Nothing more clearly reflects the interrelatedness of the Covington and Cincinnati Germans than the area of the German-American press. Due to the early development of Cincinnati in the 1830s as a center for the press, Covington never really developed in this area, but relied almost completely on the German-American press of Cincinnati, which covered events and activities in northern Kentucky. Nevertheless, there were several publications issued in Covington. Also, it was the location of one of the more significant German-American printing companies in the Greater Cincinnati area.

From 1873 to 1874, Joseph Hermes edited and published the *Gegenwart*, a weekly newspaper. From 1891-95, the *Kentucky Demokrat*, a daily newspaper was published by the Kentucky Publishing Co., and edited by J. V. Schiffer. It also issued a Sunday edition, or *Sonntagsblatt*. Circulation of this paper was more than two thousand. At the same time there were several German-American newspapers available from nearby Cincinnati, including the *Volksblatt* and the *Freie Presse*, as well as a variety of religious and special interest publications.[4]

The Alban Wolff Printing Co. Referred to earlier was one of the major German-American printing companies in the region. From 1909 to 1912, Wolff published and edited a bilingual German-English newspaper, *National-Zeitung and Volks-Zeitung - People's Friend*. The place of publication was then transferred north to Hamilton, Ohio, where it was issued under the new title *Der Deutsch-Amerikaner* by the

German-American Publishing Co. In spite of the move, Wolff continued on as editor. The newspaper basically evolved from a Covington-based publication to one with a readership which reached the Ohio Valley and beyond. Its masthead indicated that it was the "Official Paper of the German-American Alliance." It, hence, espoused and advocated the principles and philosophy as stated in the platform of the Alliance. The paper clearly can be viewed as a major organ of publication for German-American viewpoints and perspective in the region of the Greater Cincinnati area.[5]

Notes

1. Cronau, *German Achievements in America*, p. 219-23.

2. German-American national Alliance, *Protokoll der fünften Konvention des Deutsch-Amerikanischen National-Bundes der Ver. Staaten von Amerika, abgehalten vom 2. bis 6. Oktober 1909 in der Cincinnati Turnhalle zu Cincinnati, Ohio.* (Cincinnati, 1909), p. 32.

3. A collection of the works of the Wolff Printing Co. can be found in the German-Americana Collection at the University of Cincinnati. See Don Heinrich Tolzmann, *Catalog of the German-Americana Collection, University of Cincinnati.* (München: Saur, 1990), vol. 1, p.xxv. Also, see the following work at the Kenton County Public Library in Covington: *Personal Vital Records Collected from Wolff Printing Co. 1940-1989 In Alphabetical Order.* (Covington, Ky.: Wolff Printing Co., 1989).

4. Regarding the German-American press of Covington, see Karl J. J. Arndt, *The German Language Press of the Americas: Volume 1: History and Bibliography 1732-1968: United States of America.* (München: Saur, 1976), p. 168.

5. A microfilm of this paper can be found in the German-Americana Collection, Archives and Rare Books Department, University of Cincinnati.

Chapter 7

The World Wars and German-Americans

In 1885, the state of Kentucky commissioned Heinrich
Lemcke to tour the state's German-American settlements, and
to write a report for the purpose of attracting more German
immigrants to the state. He identified thirteen areas where
German-Americans had concentrated in Kentucky, the
strongest being in Louisville, Newport, and Covington.[1]
German-American life flourished in these and other areas of
the state by the turn of the century, especially as evidenced by
the many German-American churches and societies.
Involvement in political life at the state level was reflected in
the election of a German-American as governor in 1900,
William Goebel, an indication of the status and recognition
enjoyed by German-Americans.

The outbreak of the First World War struck like a bolt
of lightning from a clear blue sky. The German element was
naturally as "pro-German" as were Anglo-Americans "pro-
British." Of course, after American entrance into the war,
German-Americans did their duty, enlisting in numbers far
greater than their percentage of the population.
Unfortunately, the war brought some of the latent nativist
sympathies to the forefront, resulting in what has been
described as the anti-German hysteria.[2]

Carl Wittke has described the anti-German crusade as
"a violent, concerted, and hysterical effort to eradicate
everything of German origin in the United States. Loyal
Americans of German extraction became the victims of a

74

furor Americanus which can only be described as pathological."[3]

Name-changing, of course, became the rage, as German-Americans, their organizations, and institutions came under pressure. In Covington, this was perhaps best symbolized by Bremen St., which was changed to Pershing St., after General George Pershing, commander of the American Expeditionary Forces in Europe.[4] Name-changes were pressed by anti-German crusaders, and German-Americans yielded in an attempt to prove their patriotism. In 1918, the Covington Turngemeinde changed its name to the Covington Turners Society. Not only streets, organizations, and institutions were affected, as this was a time when family names changed too - Braun to Brown, Schmidt to Smith, Baumann to Bowman, etc.

Another way for German-Americans to attempt to prove their patriotism was to invest heavily in Liberty Bonds, i.e., war bonds. For example, in 1917 the Turners purchased $300.00 of Liberty Bonds.[5] The German heritage in general, and the German language in particular became targets in the anti-German crusade. Indeed, "Covington was a hotbed of anti-German sentiment."[6]

At Grace Church, a meeting was held 12 April 1918 "to discuss the advisability to eliminate the German services on account of the war with Germany and the general hatred of everything German by some of our fellow citizens."[7]

Anti-German rallies were held, and petitions were sent to the governor to ban German instruction in all schools, including universities. The *Kentucky Post* reported that "true Americans didn't want to expose their children to this subversive element." Placards warned against German-American newspapers at the news stands in Covington, so that soon none could be obtained except through the mail. [8] A pacifist minister from Cincinnati was brought across the river to Kentucky, where he was tied to a tree, stripped, and whipped "in the name of the women and children of Belgium."[9]

The First World War was, therefore, obviously a tragic period for German-Americans, and one which subjected them to many wrongs and injustices. Following hard on the heels of the war was prohibition. Commenting on this turn of events Karl J. Vercouteren noted: "Then to top it off, prohibition came along and shut down those most German of institutions, the breweries. Of course, home brew continued to be made in German homes, but prohibition also spelled the end of those identity-giving institutions that brought German people together - the beer garden and the social club, where Germans had kept their language and culture alive all those years."[10]

Helping people through these times was not only the strong network of families, but churches and societies. Vercouteren observes: "How did these changes affect the people? Many changes their names...It was a time when German people became quiet, conservative, and felt the need to express a 100 percent, thoroughgoing Americanism. It was the churches more than any other institution that helped carry them through the great trauma of this change. Clergy today remember the great changes int he 1960s and how difficult it was to pastor a church during those days. How much more difficult it must have been for the German pastors in the years immediately following the First World War: what tremendous changes occurred in their religious communities and their cultural communities over that time! It's to the pastors' credit that almost all of the German churches in Covington enjoyed long pastorates during that time., The story is repeated time after time of capable men who were able to carry their people through a very difficult and trying time."[11]

He also notes that "during those years, the immigrations slowed down to a mere trickle. It was a time of drawing together in the church, a focusing upon the close family ties that had always been part of the German churches, and which now sustained them."[12]

Due to the Germanophobia of the day, the National German-American Alliance folded in 1918, thus leading to the demise of what had been the major national German-American organization in American history. This meant the loss of the Alliance as an effective and influential organization. Although the societies remained, their central organization was now gone. It had also resulted in the loss of German instructional programs in the schools, and a general loss of status for things German in general. German-American tended to privatize their heritage to home, family, friends, church, and society.

The advent of the Second World War brought the U.S. into another world war against the ancestral homeland of German-Americans. Although the worst excesses of anti-Germanism were confined to the First World War, German-Americans on occasion became the subject of ethnic slurs and other kinds of harassment, and some immigrants who had not as yet attained their citizenship papers were interned for the duration of the war.

77

It should be noted that German-Americans again served in numbers greater than their percentage of the population, as they had during the First World War.[13] After the war, it would take several decades before the German heritage would again become a symbol of wide scale public pride and recognition, thereby testifying to the resiliency and strength of this heritage and its importance for the city of Covington. Ironically, the heritage which had become the target of hostility came to be recognized as that which gave Covington its distinctive character and Old World charm, and was something deserving of preservation and pride.

Notes

1. See J. Milton Grimes, "Deutsche Sprache und deutsche Einflussein Kentucky nach 1945," in: *Deutsch als Muttersprache in den USA,* Vol. 2, p. 34.

2. Regarding the first World War, see Don Heinrich Tolzmann, ed., *German-Americans and the World Wars.* (München: K. G. Saur, 1995-97).

3. Carl Wittke, *The German-Language Press in America.* (Lexington: University of Kentucky, 1957), p. 267.

4. German street names were changed elsewhere in the U.S. also. Most recently, the German street names changed in Cincinnati have received historical markers indicating what the original names were, and that they had been changed as a result of the anti-German hysteria during World War One.

5. See the *Diamond Jubilee, Covington Turners, 1855-1930.* (Covington, KY., 1977), p. 21.

6. See Karl J. Vercouteren, *The German Churches of Covington: A History of the German People and Churches of Covington, Kentucky.* (Covington, Ky., 1977), p. 21.

7. Ibid.

8. Regarding the German-American press in Kentucky, see Tolzmann, *German-Americans and the World Wars,* Vol 1, p. 186.

9. Ibid, 205.

10. Vercouteren, p. 21.

11. Ibid, p. 20.

12. Ibid, p. 21.

13. Regarding service in World War II, see Tolzmann, *German-American Soldier*, p. 328.

Chapter 8

Covington's German Heritage

Although Germans were certainly not the only group to come to Covington, they succeeded in imparting the German heritage to the image and character of the city in a way that is immediately evident to anyone coming to the city, which is also the case with a number of towns and cities across the country, but especially in the Midwest.

The Old World German heritage of its image, or *Stadtbild* is readily apparent , whether driving past Covington on I-75, and taking notice of the Bavarian Brewing Co. and Goebel Park with its distinctive *Glockenspiel*, or if driving across the Ohio River on the Roebling Suspension Bridge.

In the 1970s, the ethnic heritage and roots revival swept across the country, bringing increased interest, pride and awareness in the multi cultural diversity of America. For the German-Americans, it was the first time since before the period of the world wars that there was wide-spread recognition of the role German-Americans had played in American history. Again, there was not only interest, but public pride in the German heritage, and this often translated into an active interest in various kinds of preservation activities.[1]

In 1972, the Northern Kentucky Area Planning Commission published a housing survey, stating that many of the homes on the lower west side of Covington were in poor condition. In 1975, the city designated the area as in need of renovation. The Northern Kentucky Convention and Visitors

81

Bureau then recommended that the area would be appropriate for a German-style village within the framework of a "Rhineland of America" theme.

This took shape as the MainStrasse Village concept, which was then incorporated into the 1976 Main Street Development Plan. This aimed to improve the area bordered by the C&O Railroad on the east, by 4th St. in the north, by I-75 in the west, and by Pike St. in the south. The idea was to restore housing in the area and to establish a business district, all of which should be developed with a German heritage motif. In 1976, a $2.5 million state grant was awarded to the Northern Kentucky convention and Visitors Bureau to accomplish this goal.[2]

The MainStrasse village then began to take shape, as houses were restored and preserved, some of them sporting German flags, and as businesses, restaurants, and shops opened, many with German inscriptions and features. Also, the MainStrasse village Association began to sponsor immensely popular festivals, such as Maifest and Oktoberfest, the latter of which, it should be noted received the sponsorship of the Klostermans, an old German-American family of Covington. Other specialty events included Lunch with St. Nicholas. Two of the major motifs of the district were the Goose Girl Fountain and Goebel Park, where a beautiful *Glockenspiel* was constructed.

Other recent improvements to the city, which relate to the German heritage, was the renovation of the old Bavarian Brewing Co., which opened with a brewpub, restaurant, and party supplies in 1996.[3] The German flavor and style of these and other renovations since the 1970s is neither accidental, nor academic but rather in accordance with the German heritage of Covington - they all seem to fit in Covington. Hence, they relate to and resonate with the public, as they draw from the rich cultural heritage brought to this American Rhineland city. The fact that they do further reflects the strength of the German heritage of the area, and the depth of its roots. It should be noted that the 1990 U. S. Census indicates that 40% of the population of Covington, or 17,230 out of a total of 43,264 claim German ancestry, thereby making German-Americans the largest ethnic group in the city.[4]

Part of the German tradition has no doubt been lost or diluted as a result of two world wars, but much of the German heritage survived and weathered the storm, and has adapted well with the times. In the course of time, German-Americans have blended old and new world ways so well, that they are by and large considered as part of American life. Indeed, so much has become a basic part of everyday life that many are simply unaware of the German origins of so much of what they do, think, and say. German heritage, hence has become a part of the very fabric of life in the area. The German pioneers and their descendants have undoubtedly enriched the community of Covington, making their heritage an integral and basic part of what it is today. This is perhaps best symbolized by the creation of the MainStrasse German Village, which provides official recognition of the German dimension.

Perhaps no other event of the recent past best symbolized the re-emergence of the German heritage in Covington than the regional celebration of the German-American Day as a part of German-American Heritage Month on 6 October 1989. Sponsored by the German-American Citizens league of Greater Cincinnati, it was held at the

Cathedral Basilica of the Assumption in Covington, and included a program of Mozart and other German composers. It was noted during the program that the purpose of the celebration was "to provide the opportunity to not only celebrate the German heritage, but to also explore the many contributions and influences German-Americans have made locally and nationally."[5]

Certainly supporting the German heritage revival of the recent past have been the various preservation efforts, especially those of the MainStrasse village. Indeed, the German heritage has become not only a plus factor, but has become an attractive and highly marketable factor, especially as related not only to the tourist industry, but to area businesses, many of which have connections to Germany, or are branches of German companies.

The area's heritage has, hence, been publicized in various brochures. For example, the International Division of the Kentucky Department of Travel Development even issued a German language brochure, *Kentucky, der schöne Bluegrass Staat,* while the Convention and Visitors Bureaus of Northern Kentucky and Cincinnati also brought out a German-language brochure, *Cincinnati, U.S.A. - Northern Kentucky.* And, of course, the MainStrasse Village issues a variety of attractive flyers and brochures *auf englisch* about the Village and its numerous shops, restaurants, and special events and activities.

Hence all of the aforementioned programs and activities in Covington have worked together to bring about the gradual re-emergence of public pride and recognition of the German heritage as a basic and integral element of the city of Covington, Kentucky.

In conclusion several observations are in order. First, it is clear that the German dimension has played a major role in the history of northern Kentucky. Indeed, no history is complete, which does not include reference to such a major segment of the population. Second, it is also clear that the challenge is great to tell the story of Covington's German heritage, and the important role it has played in the history of Covington, from the beginnings to the present time. Hopefully, this work will contribute to that process.

It also should be noted that the German-American experience is an ongoing continuum, and that the German dimension in American life, like that of any ethnic heritage, is an ever-evolving part of the multi-cultural landscape that is America. What it means to be a German-American, or of any heritage, is not only an individual, but also an ever-evolving matter, which responds to the needs of the times. Scholars note that ethnic groups are constantly re-creating and re-defining themselves and ethnicity is continuously being re-invented in response to the changing realities within the ethnic group and within America society at large.[6] Ethnic heritage in general and in this case German heritage in particular is not static, but, hence, ever-evolving with the flux of times.

As German-Americans explore and express what it means to be of German heritage nationally and locally, they participate in a continuum reaching back to the beginnings of the U.S., as well as to the very beginnings of Covington, Kentucky. In this context, it is well to note the words of wisdom of Karl J. Vercouteren, formerly pastor at the Grace United Church of Christ of Covington, who observed that one's heritage forms "a foundation on which to build our lives, now in the present, and into the future."[7]

Notes

1. Regarding the ethnic heritage revival, see Dorothy and Thomas Hoobler, *The German-American Family Album.* (New York: Oxford University Pr., 1996).

2. Giglierano, p. 137.

3. For a history of the Bavarian Brewing Company, see Wimberg, pp. 6-7.

4. In Cincinnati, the population of German descent is somewhat large at ca. 50%; so that the entire Greater Cincinnati area may be viewed as one of the major German heritage centers.

5. Cited in: Don Heinrich Tolzmann, ed., *Sourcebook for the German-American Heritage Month.* (Cincinnati: German-American Studies Program, University of Cincinnati, 1991), p. iii.

6. For more recent works dealing with ethnicity in America, see Gary Gerstle, "Liberty, Coercion, and the Making of Americans," *The Journal of American History.* 84:2 (1997): 524ff; Werner Sollors, *Beyond Ethnicity: Consent and Descent in American Culture.* (New York: Oxford University Pr., 1986); Werner Sollors, *The Invention of Ethnicity.* (New York: Oxford University Pr., 1989); and Kathleen Neils Conzen, "The Invention of Ethnicity: A Perspective from the U.S.A.," *Journal of American Ethnic History.* 12(Fall 1992): 3-41; and Ormond Loomis, ed., *Cultural Conservation: The Protection of Cultural Heritage in the United States.* (Washington, D.C.: Library of Congress, 1983).

7. Vercouteren, p. 1.

86

Appendix I. Historic Sites

1. *The MainStrasse Village* - Located on the westside of Covington, the Village represents a relatively well preserved German district, which contains many shops, restaurants, saloons, gift shops, etc. The Northern Kentucky Convention and Visitors Bureau is also located here, and provides information on the district and area. Also, available is a brief introductory film on the area in English, as well as German. Special points of interest here are:

A. *The Goose Girl Fountain* - Located in the center of the Village is this fountain, commissioned by the Northern Kentucky Convention and Visitors Bureau, and completed by the Greek sculptor Elefcherious Karkadoiulias. The fountain is based on a German fairy tale by the famous Grimm brothers, "The Goose Girl."

Legend has it that the queen gave her daughter a magic handkerchief to protect her on her journey to be wed to a prince in a far away land. When stopping at a stream to water the horses, the princess dropped the handkerchief in the water, and an evil handmaiden, finding her powerless, took over the princess' horse and gown. When they arrived at the castle, the fake princess sent the real princess to a farmer saying she was a goose girl. Each day she would herd geese and at the end of the day, the goose girl would unbraid her hair and cry. One day, the farmer heard her crying and found out the truth, whereupon he took her to the king and told the whole truth of what had happened. The prince and real princess were then married and lived happily the rest of their lives, and the fake princess was imprisoned. The fountain was dedicated in October 1980.

B. *The Goebel Park* - Located on the westside of the Village, the park is a focal point, and is named in honor of William Goebel, a German-American elected Governor of Kentucky in 1900. The park contains a major tourist attraction, a Glockenspiel, which was dedicated in 1979. It is known as the Carroll Chimes Bell Tower, as it is named in honor of the then Governor of Kentucky, Julian Carroll. The German Gothic Glockenspiel plays a 43-bell carillon hourly to present mini-concerts and the lively enactment of the German folklore of the tale "The Pied Piper of Hamelin." Adjacent to the park is the Northern Kentucky Visitors Center, which provides information on the area.

C. *Pershing - Bremen St.* - Located south of the Goose Girl Fountain, just off of MainStrasse is Pershing St., which originally was Bremen St. This was one of the streets and institutions whose name was changed during the First World War due to the anti-German hysteria of the time.

2. *Sites Adjacent to MainStrasse Village* - there are a number of sites of interest located adjacent, or nearby the German Village, including:

A. *Mutter Gottes Kirche/Mother of God Church* - Located at 119 W. 6th St., this church was built by the German Catholics of Covington in 1842 with funds from the Leopoldine Mission Society of Vienna. Considered the most beautiful German-American church in the Greater Cincinnati area, it contains five murals by the German-American artist, Johann Schmitt, who trained Duveneck. The large, stained-glass windows at the ends of the transept were imported from Munich in 1890. The one on the left depicts the Immaculate Conception and the one at the right the Assumption. The art windows along the sides of the church for the most part

89

represent Old Testament promises in the lower panels and their New Testament fulfillment in the upper panels.

The decorative frescoes by Wenceslaus Thien, another German-American artist, are noted for their design and color harmony. The artistry of Krienhagen above the windows expresses symbolism from the Litany of Loretto. The large crucifix behind the main alter was the work of the Covington German sculptor, Ferdinand Muer, and was blessed in 1871, and originally installed at the communion rail. The Stations of the Cross were done by Paul Deschwanden in 1872. The tower clocks were installed in 1875 and are 110 feet from the floor, and are 8 feet in diameter. The organ, installed in 1876, was made by A. Koehnken and Grimm, and considered one of the finest in the west.

The brother-pastors, William and Henry Tappert are buried at the alter of our Lady of Perpetual Help at the right rear of the church. Oil paintings of them hang in the choir loft. The picture of our Lady of Perpetual Help at the alter was received by Fr. William Tappert from Pope Leo XIII in private audience, 22 August 1882. The wooden carved alters are the work of Henry and Frederick Schroeder, and the communion table and pulpit are the work of Donnenfelser.

The church was consecrated in 1903, and the main marble alter was constructed in anticipation of the consecration and a mosaic English cut tile floor laid around it. The twelve marble crosses along the sides of the church were placed for the ceremony in conformance with the requirements of the consecration. A lighted candle placed over each at the beginning of the service represents the twelve apostles - the "light of the world."

The German Mettlach tile main and side aisles were laid in 1921, the same year in which the Carrara angels with holy water bowls in the back of the church were given to the parish. The marble baptistry at the left rear of the church was added in 1929. The stone statues of SS. Peter and Paul and the two mythological lions in front of the church were completed at the Mayer Royal Art Institute in Munich.

B. *Grace United Church of Christ* - Located at Lockwood and Willard St., this building of this German Reformed Church was dedicated in 1863, but during the First World War changed its name to the Grace Reformed Church due to the anti-Germanism of the time. It is now part of the United church of Christ. Note the historic marker in the front of the church.

C. *The Turner Hall* - Located at 447 Pike St., this hall was built in 1877 by the Covington Turners, the oldest German-American society in Covington, which was founded in 1855.

D. *The Bavarian Brewing Company* - Located just south of the MainStrasse village, the Bavarian Brewing Company began as the Deglow Brewing Co. in 1866. It became the Bavarian Brewing Company in 1870, and under the direction of William Riedlin, it became a major brewery. By 1896, it produced 32,000 barrels of beer annually. In 1934, the brewery re-opened after prohibition, and continued operation into the 1960s. In 1996 it re-opened after extensive renovation as a brewpub, restaurant and party store. Its location alongside I-75 contributes effectively to presenting the German heritage of Covington to passers-by.

E. *Glier's Meats, Inc.* - Located at 533 W. 11th St., Glier's is the worlds largest producer of goetta, a regionally popular German sausage.

F. *The Behringer-Crawford Museum* - Located west of the village in Devou Park, the museum promoted local history and heritage through its exhibits and programs, and also contains a library focusing on the region.

3. *The Riverfront Area* - Among the sites in this area, the most notable are:

A. *The John A. Roebling Suspension Bridge* - Completed in 1867, the bridge is a veritable symbol of the entire Greater Cincinnati area, and connects Covington and Cincinnati. It is considered Roebling's model for his world-famous Brooklyn Bridge, which was completed after this bridge. Widely viewed as an architectural and historic landmark, it is also considered symbolic of the area - a bridge built by a German immigrant, Johann August Roebling. The bridge was completed on New Year's Day 1867. It cost ca. $1.8 million to build and measures 1,057 feet between the 230 foot high towers, and 1,619 feet between the shore anchors. The bridge was placed on the national register of historic places in 1975, and illuminated with lights in 1984 in honor of Julia Langsam, president of the Covington and Cincinnati Bridge Co. And wife of Dr. Walter Langsam, president of the University of Cincinnati, as well as a well-known German-American historian.

B. *The Roebling Monument* - Located at the foot of the bridge at its southeast corner, is a statue depicting Roebling, which bears the following inscription: "From an Immigrant to an Immigrant. John A. Roebling and to all

Immigrants who have helped build Greater Cincinnati, from Matth. Toebben and his family." Note that the funds for the monument came from a well-known German-American in the construction industry in northern Kentucky, Matth. Toebben.

C. *The Amos Shinkle Townhouse* - Located at 210 Garrard St., this townhouse belonged to the Covington German, Amos Shinkle (1811-92), who was a leading businessman in the area, and who was the major promoter of the Roebling Suspension Bridge, and president of the Covington and Cincinnati Bridge Co. The home, a two-story brick townhouse, was built in 1854 and described by a columnist as follows: "Mr. Shinkle is one of our most enterprising businessmen, and in arranging for this building seems to have been actuated by a determination to combine elegance and convenience, regardless of cost."

D. *Shinkle's Row* - Shinkle built an entire series of seven townhouses located at 230-242 East 2nd St. This row of Renaissance Revival townhouses was his largest residential building project, and was restored in the mid-1970s.

E. *The Ernst Home* - Located at 401 Garrard St. this home belonged to the Pennsylvania German banker, William Ernst (1813-95), who served as president of the Northern Bank of Kentucky, located at Each 3rd St. and Scott Boulevard. His son, John P. Ernst, also served as president of the bank but resigned to become president of the family's other bank, the German National Bank, located on Madison Ave.

F. *The Wolff Printing Co.* - Located at the corner of Court St. and Greenup St., this building housed the office of one of the major German-American printing companies in the

Greater Cincinnati area, which printed materials in German and English for the greater part of the century.

4. *Sites South of the Riverfront* - Directly south of the riverfront area there are the following sites:

a. *The Duveneck Home* - Located at 1226 Greenup St., this was the home of Frank Duveneck (1848-1919), considered the premier German-American artist of the area. After having been apprenticed to Covington's Institute of Catholic Art, he went to Munich in 1869, where he studied at the Royal Academy of Fine Arts. After living in various places in Europe and America, he accepted a permanent appointment in 1900 at the Art Academy of Cincinnati. It was said that he was the greatest painter of his generation, and his influence was extensive due to his many students.

B. *The Cathedral Basilica* - Located on Maidson Ave. Between 11th and 12th St., this church was modeled after Notre Dame, and contains the works of German and German-American artists. Mayer & Co. Of Munich produced the stained-glass windows on the lower and clerestory levels. Four murals for the chaoel and a triptych on the east wall were donated by Frank Duveneck. The well-known German-American sculptor, Clement Barnhorn, produced the statue of the Madonna and the carving of the Assumption of Mary above the front door of the cathedral.

C. *The Odd Fellows Hall* - Located at 434-440 Madison Ave., this has been a Covington landmark since its dedication in 1857, and was designed by the Pennsylvania German Gedge Brothers and Co. Amos Shinkle, a member of the Odd Fellows was partly responsible for the construction of the building and due to his connections with Roebling, it is thought that the bridge builder was responsible for the suspension of the upper floors of the building. The hall itself was the location of civic, cultural, and social events.

5. *The Southside of Covington* - Expecially noteworthy on the southside of Covington is the Mother of God Church Cemetery, located on Madison Pike. The cemetery contains numerous beautiful monuments, many of them carved with German insriptions, as well as the following noteworthy sites:

A. *Ich bin die Auferstehung und das Lebin-I am the Resurrection and the Life* - This magnificent religious monument was created by the German-American sculptor, Clement H. Barnhorn, and was dedicated in May 1915.

B. *The Kühr Monument* - Located near Barnhorn's statue is the final resting place of Fr. Kürr, the founding father of the Mutter Gottes Kirche. Also nearby are the resting places of other members of the clergy.

C. *The Duveneck Monument* - A beautiful monument marks the grave ot the German-American artist, Frank Duveneck, and other members of his family.

Appendix II. The German Pioneer Society

The founding officers of the Society in 1877 were: Georg Welling, president; Henry Deglow, vice-president; B. H. F. Hellebusch, secretary; Henry Adams, treasurer; and the following were board members: Conrad Deisler, John Herold, G. H. Schleutker, Victor Engert, and B. Marschall. The founding members were:

1. Conrad Ackermann, born 16 October 1826 in Doerzbach an der Jaxt, Württemberg, emigrated in 1848.

2. Heinrich Adams, born 5 October 1823 in Schönstein, Reg. Bez. Koblentz, Prussia, emigrated in 1847.

3. Georg Johann Albrinck, born 10 October 1821 in Löningen, Oldenburg, emigrated in 1845.

4. Herman Arlinghaus, born 21 June 1822 in Dinklage, Amt Steinfeld, Oldenburg, emigrated 1849.

5. Karl Asmann, born 29 September 1831 in Hanau, Kurhessen, emigrated in 1852.

6. Nicolaus Bath, born 21 November 1836 in Schweyen, Lothringen, emigrated 1853.

7. Georg Bernhard, born 7 March 1828 in Utterichshausen, Amt Schwarzenfels, Kurhessen, emigrated in 1830.

8. Heinrich Berte, born 10 December 1820 in Holdorf, Amt Damme, Oldenburg, emigrated in 1837.

9. Joseph Birkle, born 19 December 1808 in Benzinger, Hohenzollern Sigmaringen, emigrated in 1849.

10. Johann Herman Blau, M.D., born 18 May 1832 in Vehringendorf, Hohenzollern-Sigmaringen, emigrated in 1857.

11. Moritz Bleyer, born October 1821 in Prichowitz, Bohemia, emigrated in 1848.

12. Karl Bogenschütz, born 30 June 1820 in Sickingen, Hohenzollern-Hechingen, emigrated in 1843.

13. Johan Bosche, born 12 January 1824 in Lutten, Amt Vechta, Oldenburg, emigrated in 1847.

14. Johann Gerhard Clemens Bramlage, born in 1823 in Lohne, Amt Steinfeld, Oldenburg, emigrated in 1848.

15. Albert Britzwein, born 28 October 1830 in Braunschweig, emigrated in 1853.

16. Johann Joseph Busse, born 1 May 1836 in Goldenstedt, Amt Vechta, Oldenburg, emigrated in 1846.

17. Herman Rudolph Deglow, born 4 January 1828 in Lippehne, Kreis Solden, Reg. -Bez. Frankfurt a.d. Oder, Prussia, emigrated in 1851.

18. Conrad Deisler, born 6 January 1824 in Assamstadt, Oberamt Bocksberg, Baden, emigrated in 1849.

19. Johann Christian Dorsel, born 29 December 1833 in Mauritz bei Münster, Westfalen, emigrated in 1854.

20. Bernhard Dreesmann, born 29 November 1814 in Alfhausen, Amt Bersenbrück, Hannover, emigrated in 1839.

21. Heinrich Dreesmann, born 18 December 1822 in Alfhausen, Hannover, emigrated in 1840.

22. Ignatius Droege, born 30 January 1828 in Velmede, Reg. -Bez. Arensberg, Westfalen, emigrated in 1849.

23. Lorenz Droege, born 24 June 1825 in Velmede, emigrated in 1853.

24. Joseph Duveneck, born 24 May 1824 in Visbeck, Amt Vechtha, Oldenburg, emigrated in 1848; the step-father of the well-known artist, Frank Duveneck.

25. Wilhelm Eifert, born 18 February 1825 in Sickendorf, Hessen-Darmstadt, emigrated in 1849.

26. Wilhelm Eilers, born 1 July 1826 in Sögel, Amt Hümeling, Hannover, emigrated in 1847.

27. Johann Eisele, born 19 May 1831 in Oettingen, Oberamt Kirchheim, Württemberg, emigrated in 1856.

28. Victor Caspar Engert, born 31 March in Sommerach, Bavaria, emigrated in 1834.

29. Franz Feldkamp, born 18 January 1837 in Alfhausen, Hannover, emigrated in 1854.

30. Wilhelm David Feuss, born 26 May 1834 in Brinkum, Hannover, emigrated in 1848.

31. Felix Fritz, born 18 May 1826 in Buchheim, Amt Stockach, Baden, emigrated in 1845.

32. Bernard Gatenberg, born 30 June 1821 in Bochum, Prussia, emigrated in 1848.

33. Carl Geisbauer, born in Lorenzen in Elsass, emigrated in 1830.

34. Johann Adam Geiswein, born 6 April 1837 in Eschenstruh bei Kassel, Kurhessen, emigrated in 1847.

35. Wilhelm Göbel, born 10 June 1831 in Göttingen, Hannover, emigrated in 1854.

36. Friedrich Goerdes, born 29 October 1815 in Arnsberg, Prussia, emigrataed in 1849.

37. Anton Haake, born 12 September 1820 in Endorf, Kreis Arensberg, Prussia, emigrated in 1845.

38. Johann Hasemeyer, born 10 February 1828 in Essingen, Rheinpfalz, Bavaria, emigrated in 1852.

39. Heinrich Henn, born 8 December 1831 in Rothenbach, Reinpfalz, Bavaria, emigrated in 1850.

40. Joseph Hermes, born 1 November 1834 in Ostendorpp, Westfalen, emigrated in 1853.

41. Friedrich Wilhelm Heckmann, born 6 September 1820 in Hamburg, emigrated in 1839.

42. Bernard Hermann Hegge, born 19 Arpil 1823 in Beesten, Amt Freren, Hannover, emigrated in 1850.

43. Johann Heinrich Heile, born 3 March 1818 in Delinghausen, Merzen, Amt Fürstenau, Hannover, emigrated in 1850.

44. B. H. F. Hellebusch, born 28 April 1825 in Borringhausen bei Damme, Oldenburg, served as a priest at the Mutter Gottes Kirche, and was the author of religious and devotional literature.

45. Bernard Hewing, born 8 June 1830 in Ochtrup, Westfalia, emigrated in 1833.

46. Franz Höne, born 11 August 1811 in Dinklage, Oldenburg, emigrated in 1845.

47. Wilhelm Holtmann, born 1 November 1824 in Altenberge, Kreis Münster, Prussia, emigrated in 1852.

48. Georg Kampe, born 3 December 1832 in Brenna, Kurhessen, emigrated in 1850.

49. Johann Kappel, born 1 January 1831 in Oelbrunn, Oberamt, Maulbronn, Württemberg, emigrated in 1854.

50. Heinrich Kentrup, born 6 February 1820 in Amelsbüren, Kreis Münster, Westfalen, emigrated in 1847.

51. Fritz Kleist, born 28 March 1827 in Soest, Westfalen, emigrated in 1854.

52. Johann Bernhard Klostermann, born 29 January 1837 in Hannover, emigrated in 1847; ancestor of the family which founded the well-known baking company, and now sponsors the annual Covington Oktoberfest.

53. Franz Knoll, born 13 March 1829 in Herxheim bei Landau, Babaria, emigrated in 1846.

54. Georg Knorr, born 9 December 1832 in Baldersheim, Bavaria, emigrated in 1853.

55. Clemens Köbbe, born 22 August 1827 in Lenerich a.d. Wallage, Hannover, emigrated in 1840.

56. Georg B. F. Köhler, born 8 February 1823 in Waldersprick, Kurhessen, emigrated in 1846.

57. Karl Lang, born 20 March in Saar-Union in Elsass, emigrated in 1854.

58. B. Otto Lots, born 11 July 1830 in Altenburg, Sachsen-Altenburg, emigrated in 1846; served in the Mexican War.

59. Bernhard Marschall, born 7 March 1816 in Sögel, Hannover, emigrated in 1847.

60. Johann Bernard Meibers, born 21 August in Esterwege, Amt Sögel, Hannover, emigrated in 1852.

61. Wilhelm Adam Menniger, born 24 January 1832 in Heldenberg, Hessen-Darmstadt, emigrated in 1843.

62. Johann Heinrich Meyer, born 15 September 1818 in Kappel, Amt Kloppenburg, Oldenburg, emigrated in 1837.

63. Johann Hermann Middendorf, born 17 April 1837 in Amt Sögel, Hannover, emigrated in 1851.

64. Wilhelm Middendorf, born 17 Arpil 1837 in Amt Sögel, Hannover, emigrated in 1851.

65. Heinrich Mönkedick, born 15 February 1824 in Damme, Oldenburg, emigrated in 1849.

66. Heinrich Moselage, born 26 December 1828 in Westkirchen, Kreis Münster, Westfalen, emigrated in 1857.

67. Ferdinand Nienaber, born 3 January 1829 in Haverbeck, Amt Damme, Oldenburg, emigrated in 1851.

68. Bernard Heinrich Nipper, born 3 January 1820 in Lastrop, Oldenburg, emigrated in 1851.

69. Conrad Paul, born 28 February 1826, in Nidda bei Worms, emigrated in 1853.

70. Hermann Heinrich Joseph Puthoff, born 22 August 1833 in Kettenkamp, Ankum Hannover, emigrated in 1839.

71. Johann Rehfuss, born 15 November 1823 in Dorhen, Kreis Schwarzwald, Württemberg, emigrated in 1848.

72. Heinrich Reisloh, born 23 December 1822 in Münden, Hannover, emigrated in 1851.

73. Georg Jacob Renner, born 11 February 1822 in Dannstadt, Rheinpfalz, Bavaria, emigrated in 1849.

74. Franz Heinrich Rotert, born 3 October 1818 in Rulle, Amt Osnabrück, Hannover, emigrated in 1839.

75. Jacob Friedrich Rothenhöfer, born 13 September 1832 in Horrheimk, Oberamt Vaichingen a.d. Enz., emigrated in 1854.

76. Joseph Rusche, born 23 December 1825 in Amt Damme, Oldenburg, emigrated in 1847.

77. Friedrich Heinrich Sandmann, born 1 February 1823 in Hemsloh, Amt Diepholz, Hannover, emigrated in 1844.

78. Heinrich Wilhelm Schleutker, born 4 March in Lengerich, Kreis Tecklenburg, Westfalen, emigrated in 1845.

79. Gerhard Heinrich Schleutker, born 5 November 1836 in Lengerich, Kreis Tecklenburg, Westfalen, emigrated in 1845.

80. Anton Schnorr, born 13 August 1834 in Wildesgheim, Kreis Kreutznach, Prussia, emigrated in 1853.

81. Johannes Schöttle, born 5 February 1830 in Ebhausen, Württemberg, emigrated in 1847.

82. Heinrich Schlöttler, born 13 December 1824 in Recklinghausen, Westfalen, emigrated in 1846.

83. Georg Schorr, born 15 June 1819 in Bergostheim, Bavaria, emigrated in 1854.

84. Augustin Schuler, born 15 October 1827 in Müs, Kurfürstentum Hessen, emigrated in 1847.

85. Mathias Schwarz, born 26 February 1831 in Hausen, Hohenzollern-Hechingen, emigrated in 1850.

86. Michael Schweier, born 23 March 1828 in Mindesheim, Elsass, emigrated in 1846.

87. Herman Heinrich Schwertmann, born 14 December 1819 in Althausen, Hannover, emigrated in 1856.

88. Theodor Sehlhorst, born 8 December 1826 in Rheine, Westfalen, emigrated in 1851.

89. Heinrich Spenneberg, born 24 June 1818 in Sierhausen, Amt Damme, Oldenburg, emigrated in 1846.

90. Franz Joseph Stallo, born 9 January 1818 in Sierhausen, Amt Damme, Oldenburg, emigrated in 1846.

91. Johannes Staut, born 27 May 1826 in Doerzbach, Oberamt Künzelsau, Württemberg, emigrated in 1848.

92. Conrad Stein, born 8 February in Binder, Amt Wohldenberg, Hannover, emigrated in 1852.

93. Fidel Stöckle, born 11 July 1831 in Veringersdorf, Hohenzollern-Sigmaringen, emigrated in 1854.

94. Leonhard Stoll, born 10 September 1818 in Mühlhausen, Elsass, emigrated in 1844.

95. Gottfried Supple, born 28 October 1836 in Weilersbach, Amt Fillingen, Baden, emigratee in 1854.

96. Peter Teipel, born 6 March 1821 in Niederfeld, Reg.-Bez. Arnsberg, Prussia, emigrated in 1847.

97. Heinrich Terlau, born 4 October 1827 in Borghorst, Westfalen, emigrated in 1852.

98. Heinrich August Theissen, born 11 August 1828 in Halverde bei Hopsten, Westfalen, emigrated in 1847.

99. Franz Eduard Thoss, born 17 January 1807 in Langenweisendorf, Schleiz, emigrated in 1836.

100. Karl Ulrich, born 5 May in Kleinbockenheim, Rheinpfalz, Bavaria, emigrated in 1847.

101. Gottfried Walt, born 29 December 1825 in Ebshausen, Oberamt Nagold, Württemberg, emigrated in 1854.

102. Heinrich Warnke, born 25 December 1819 in Wittstedt, Amt Iburg, Hannover, emigrated in 1845.

103. Georg Welling, born in Widendorla bei Mühlhausen, Thüringen, and emigrated in 1847.

104. Heinrich Wesemann, born 20 January in Blumberg, Lippe-Detmold, emigrated in 1856.

105. Anton Wiechmann, born 4 November 1817 in Bunnen, Amt Löningen, Oldenburg, emigrated in 1835.

106. Wilhelm Willen, born 29 October 1807 in Evankamp, Löningen, Oldenburg, emigrated in 1835.

107. Joseph Wördemann, born 13 March 1833 in Neuenkirchen, Amt Damme, Oldenburg, emigrated in 1856.

108. Johann Würth, born 24 October 1820 in Pflugfeld, Oberamt Ludwigsburg, Württemberg, emigrated in 1848.

109. G. A. Zwick, born 14 March 1836 in Württemberg, emigrated in 1847.

Selective Bibliography

Adams, Willi Paul. *The German -Americans: An Ethnic Experience.* Translated and adapted by LaVern J. Rippley and Eberhard Reichmann. (Indianapolis: Max Kade German-American Center, Indiana University-Purdue University at Indianapolis, 1993).

Ahmann, Ignatius M. *Parochial Symphony of St. Aloysius Church.* (Cincinnati: Press of Schulte & Cappel, 1909).

Armorial de la Generalite D'Alsace. (Paris, Comar & Strassburg, 1861).

Arndt, Karl J. R. *The German Language Press of the Americas: Volume 1: History and Bibliography, 1732-1968.* (München: Saur, 1976).

Barry, Colman. *The Catholic Church and German--Americans.* (Milwaukee: Bruce, 1953).

Baughin, William A. "Nativism in Cincinnati Before 1860," (M.A. Thesis, University of Cincinnati, 1863).

Becker, Carl M. *The Village: A History of Germantown, Ohio, 1804-1976.* (Germantown, Ohio: Historical Society of Germantown, 1981).

Billington, Ray Allen. *The Protestant Crusade, 1800-1860: A Study of the Origins of American Nativism.* (Chicago: Quadrangle Books, 1964).

Boh, John H. and Howard W. Boehmker. *Walking Tour of Westside Covington, Ky.* (Cincinnati: Cincinnati Historical Society).

Brungs, Mary Camelite. *The Church of the Mother of God: A Centennial Chronicle* (Covington, Ky.: Jameson-Rolfes, 1941).

Butterfield, C. W. *The Washington Letters-Crawford Letters.* (Cincinnati: Robert Clark & Co., 1877).

Cassel, Daniel Kolb. *A Genea-Biographical History of the Rittenhouse Family and all its Branches in America, with Sketches of their Descendants, from the Earliest Available Records to the Present Time.* (Philadelphia: The Rittenhouse Memorial Association, 1893 Collins, Lewis. *Collins' Historical Sketches of Kentucky* 2nd ed. (Covington, Ky.: collins & Co., 1874).

Cincinnati Art Museum. *Exhibition of the Work of Frank Duveneck, May 23 through June 21, 1936.* (Cincinnati: Cincinnati Art Museum, 1936).

Covington. Economic Development Department. *Bavarian Brewery Redevelopment Project: Urban Renewal Plan, City of Covington, Kentucky, August, 1996.* (Covington" Economic Development Department, City of covington, 1996).

Covington Turners. *Diamond Jubileee, Covington Turners, 1855-1930.* (Covington: Wolff's Standard Printing Works, 1930).

_____. *One Hundredth Anniversary Program of the Covington Turners' Society, 1855-1955.* (Covington, Ky.: Wolff's Standard Printing Works, 1955).

Cronau, Rudolf. *German Achievements in America: Rudolf Cronau's Survey History.* Edited by Don Heinrich Tolzmann. (Bowie, MD: Heritage Books, Inc., 1995).

Deutsche Schuetzen-Gesellschaft of Covington. *Official Souivenir, 28th Annual Crowning Fest of the Deutsche Schuetzen-Gesellschaft of Covington, Ky., 1882-1910.* (Cincinnati: Hennegan, 1910).

Douglass, Paul. *The Story of German Methodism: Biography of An Immigrant Soul.* (New York: The Methodist Books Concern, 1939).

Faust, Albert B. *The German Element in the U.S.* (New York: Steuben Society of America, 1927).

Findsen, Owen. "Riots Disrupted But Couldn't Sway Election," *Cincinnati Enquirer.* (10 March 1996).

Ford, Edward, *David Rittenhouse, Astronomer-Patriot, 1732-1796.* (Philadelphia: University of Pennsylvania Pr., 1946).

Fox, Clifford H. *German Presbyterianism in the Upper Mississippi Valley.* (Ypsilianti, Michigan: University Lithographers, 1942).

Freiberg, Walter A. *A Guide to the Cathedral.* (Covington, Ky.: The Messenger Publishing Co., 1947).

Ganz neuer Westlicher für die Staaten von Ohio, Kentucky und Indiana, besonders eingerichtete Calender auf das Jahr. . . 1818. (Lancaster, Ohio: Johann Hermann, 1817).

German Pioneer Society of Covington. *German Pioneer Society of Covington, Ky., 1877-1902.* (Covington, Ky.: Kenton County Public Library, 1988).

German Pioneer Society of Covington. *Gedenkblatt zum 25-jaehrigen Jubilaeum des Deutschen Pionier-Vereins von Covington, Ky., gehalten am Montag, 9. Juni 1902.* (Covington, Ky.: Wolff's Standard Printing Works, 1902).

German-American National Alliance. *Protokoll der fünften Konvention des Deutsch-Amerikanischen Naitonal-Bundes der Ver. Staaten von Amerika, abgehalten vom 2. bis 6. Oktober 1909 in der Cincinnati Turnhalle zu Cincinnati, Ohio.* (Cincinnati, 1909).

Giglierano, Geoffrey J. et al, *The Bicentennial Guide to Greater Cincinnati: A Portrait of Two Hundred Years.* (Cincinnati: Cincinnati Historical Society, 1988).

Grimes, J. Milton. "Deutsche Sprache und deutsche Einflüsse in Kentucky nach 1945," in: *Deutsch als Muttersprache in den Vereinigten Staaten.* (Wiesbaden: Steiner, 1985), Vol. II, pp.

Heermann, Norbert. *Frank Duveneck.* (Boston: Houghton Mifflin Co., 1918).

Hellebusch, B. H. F. *Katholisches Gesang- und Gebet-Buch: Eine Auswahl der vorzüglichsten Chorale und Kirchenlieder, für zwei Stimmen gesetzt, mit den gowöhnlichen Andachtsübungen.* 69. Aufl. (New York: Benziger, 1874).

Hurley, Daniel. *Cincinnati: The Queen City.* (Cincinnati: Cincinnati Historical Society, 1982).

Kercheval, Samuel. *A History of the Valley of Virginia.* 2nd ed. (Woodstock, VA: J. Gatewood, 1850).

Klauprecht, Emil. *Cincinnati, or, The Mysteries of the West: Emil Klauprecht's German-American Novel.* Translated by Steven Rowan and edited by Don Heinrich Tolzmann. (New York: Peter Lang, 1996).

_____. *German Chronicle in the History of the Ohio Valley and its Capital City, Cincinnati, in Particular.* (Translated by Dale V. Lally, and edited by Don Heinrich Tolzmann. (Bowie, MD: Heritage Books, Inc., 1992).

Kleber, John E., ed., *The Kentucky Encyclopeida.* (Lexington, Ky.: University Press of Kentucky, 1992).

Leighly, John. *German Family Names in Kentucky Place Names.* (New York: American Name Society, 1983).

McGann, Agnes. "Nativism in Kentucky in 1860," (M.A. Thesis, Catholic University of America, 1944).

McSherry, James. *A History of Maryland.* (Baltimore: J. Murphy & Co., 1850).

Neuhaus, Robert. *Unsuspected Genius: The Art and Life of Frank Duveneck.* (San Francisco: Bedford Pr., 1987).

Nordhoff, Charles. *Northern California, Oregon, and the Sandwich Islands.* (London: Sampson Low, Marston, Low & Searle, 1874).

Ott, Franziska. *The Anti-German Hysteria: German-American Life on the Home Front, An Exhibit in Commemoration of the 1994 Prager Memorial Day, April 5, University of Cincinnati Blegen Library, March 15 to April 15, 1994.* (Cincinnati: University of Cincinnati Libraries, 1994).

Pohlkamp, Diomede. *A Franciscan Artist of Kentucky: Life of Artist Johann Schmitt, 1825-1898.* (St. Bonaventura, NY: Reprint of Franciscan Studies, June 1947), pp. 147-70.

Pumroy, Eric and Katja Rampelmann, *Research Guide to the Turner Movement in the United States.* (Westport, Conn.: Greenwood Pr., 1996).

Rattermann, H. A. "Die deutschen Pioniere von Kenton County, Kentucky," *Der Deutsche Pionier.*9(1877):258-64, 309-15, 352-57.

_____. "Kurze historische Skizze der Deutschen Vereinigten Evangelischen St. Paul-Gemeinde in Covington, Ky.," *Der Deutsche Pionier.* 18(1886): 352-53.

_____. Zwei deutsche Ehrenmänner," *Der Deutsche Pionier.* 10(1878): 298-308.

Ryan, Paul E. *History of the Diocese of Covington, Kentucky: On the Occasion of the Centenary of the Diocese, 1853-1953.* (Covington, Ky., 1954).

St. Aloysius Church of Covington. *Historical Sketch of St. Aloysius Church, Covington, Kentucky: Diamond Jubilee Celebration, 1865-1940.* (Covington: Alban Wolff, 1933).

_____. *The St. Aloysius Congregation: Financial Report, Nineteen Hundred and Thirty-Two.* (Covington: Alban Wolff, 1933).

St. Georgius Jung-Männer-Unterstützungs-Verein of Covington. *Gedenkblatt zur Feier des 25-jährigen Jubiläums des St. Georgius Jung-Männer-Unterstützungs-Vereins.* (Covington, 1897).

St Paul Methodist Church of Cincinnati. *Centennial Souvenir: In Honor of the Three Conferences Meeting in Cincinnati and Covington, and the Commencement of Volume III of the Chimes: Cincinnati Annual Conference, Wesley Chapel, Sept. 2, 1903, Central German Annual Conference, Third German Methodist Church, Sept 9, 1903, Kentucky Annual Conference, Union Methodist Church, Covington, Kentucky, 1903.* (Cincinnati: St. Paul's Methodist Church, 1903).

St. Paul's Evangelical/Protestant Church of Covington. *Gedenkschrift zur 50-jährigen Jubel-Feier der Evang.-Prot. St. Paulus Kirche zu Covington, Ky. am 29. August 1897.* (Covington, Ky.: Covington Printing Works, 1897)

Schulte, Edward J. *The Lord Was My Client.* (Privately printed, n.d.)

Schuricht, Hermann. *The German Element in Virginia: Hermann Schuricht's History.* Edited by Don Heinrich Tolzmann. (Bowie, MD: Heritage Books, Inc., 1993).

114

Silberstein, Iola Hessler. *Cincinnati, Then and Now.* (Cincinnati: The League of Women Voters of the Cincinnati Area, 1982).

Smith, Allen Webb. *Beginning at "The Point": A Documented History of Northern Kentucky and Environs, The Town of Covington in Particular, 1751-1834.* (Park Hills, Ky.: Smith, 1977).

Smith, Clifford N. *Early Nineteenth Century German Settlers in Ohio (mainly Cincinnati and Environs), Kentucky, and other States.* (McNeal, Ariz.: Westland Publications, 1984).

Spanheimer, Mary Edmund. *Heinrich Armin Rattermann, German-American Author, Poet, and Historian, 1832-1923.* (Washington, D.C.: The Catholic University of America, 1937).

Stierlin, Ludwig. *Der Staat Kentucky und die Stadt Louisville, mit besonderer Berücksichtigung des deutschen Elements.* (Louisville: Louisville Anzeiger, 1873).

Tenkotte, Paul Allen. *A Heritage of Art and Faith: Downtown Covington Chruches.* (Covington, Ky.: Kenton County Historical Society, 1986).

_____. "Rival Cities to Suburb: Covington and Newport, Kentucky, 1790-1890," (Ph.D., Diss., University of Cincinnati, 1989).

Tolzmann, Don Heinrich. *Abraham Lincoln's Ancestry: German or English?: M.D. Learned's Investigatory History.* (Bowie, MD: Heritage Books, Inc., 1993).

_____. *Catalog of the German-American Collection, University of Cincinnati*. (München: Saur, 1990).

_____. *Cincinnati's German Heritage*. (Bowie, MD: Heritage Books, Inc., 1994).

_____. *Festschrift for the German-American Tricentennial Jubilee, Cincinnati 1983*. (Cincinnati: Cincinnati Historical Society, 1982).

_____. *The First Description of Cincinnati and other Ohio Settlements: The Travel Report of Johann Heckewelder (1792): With an Introduction by H. A. Rattermann*. (Lanham, MD: University Press of America, 1988).

_____. *German Pioneer Life: A Social History*. (Bowie, MD: Heritage Books, Inc., 1992).

_____. *The German-American Forty-Eighters, 1848-1998*. (Indianapolis: Max Kade German-American Center & Indiana German Heritage Society, 1998).

_____. *German-American Literature*. (Metuchen, NJ: Scarecrow Pr., 1977).

_____. *The German-American Soldier: J.G. Rosengarten's Survey History*. (Bowie, MD: Heritage Books, Inc., 1996).

_____. *German-Americana: A Bibliography*. (Metuchen, NJ: Scarecrow Pr., 1975).

_____. *German-Americans in the World Wars*. (München: Saur, 1995-97).

_____. *Ohio Valley German Biographical Index: A Supplement.* (Bowie, MD: Heritge Books, Inc., 1993).

_____. *Das Ohiotal - The Ohio Valley: The German Dimension.* (New York: Peter Lang, 1993).

_____. "150th Anniversary - The Cincinnati Central Turners," *Society for German-American Studies Newsletter.* 18:3(1997): 18-19.

Vercouteren, Karl J. *The German Churches of Covington: A History of The German People and Churches of Covington, Kentucky.* (Covington, Ky., 1997).

Wimberg, Robert J. *Cincinnati Breweries.* (Cincinnati: The Ohio Book Store, 1989).

Wittke, Carl. *The German-Language Press of America.* (Lexington: University Press of Kentucky, 1957).

Wolff Printing Co. *Personal Vital Records Collected from Wolff Printing Co., 1940-1989 in Alphabetical Order.* (Covington, Ky.: Wolff Printing Co., 1989).

Zucker, A. E. *The Forty-Eighters: Political Refugees of the German Revolution of 1848.* (New York: Columbia University Pr., 1950).

Index of Names

Ackermann, Conrad, 96
  Mrs. Conrad, 52
  Heinrich, 29, 30,
Adams, Heinrich, 96
  Henry, 51, 96
  Willi Paul, 46, 108
Affal, Michael, 20
Ahmann, Ignatius M.,
  108
Albers, H. H., 56, 68
Albrinck, Georg
  Johann,96
Allgaier, Michael, 22
Ante, Adolph, 69
Arlinghaus, Herman, 96
Arndt, J. R., 73, 108
Asimus, Gottlieb, 71
Asmann, Karl, 96
Averbeck, Frank A., 68
Bach, Joseph, 30
Ballinger, Johann, 30
Barnhorn, Clement, 94,
  95
Barry, Colman, 108
  James, 36
Bath, Nicolaus, 96
Baughin, William A.,
  46, 108
Baumann, Georg, 11
  Johann 8

Bechtold, Paul, 69
Becker, Carl M., 26, 108
Bedinger, Benjamin F.,
  9, 30
  Georg Michael, 8
Behle, Bernhard 22
  Carl, 69
Behringer-Crawford
  Museum, 92
Benike, Arnold, 30
Benton, Mortimer M., 14
Berling, Herman, 70
Bernhard, Georg, 23, 96
Berns, Barney, 69
Berte, Heinrich, 23, 96
Berti, Henri, 53
Bertlinger, Bernard, 30
Billington, Ray Allen, 46,
  108
Binz, Henry, 68
Birkle, Joseph, 97
  Mathias, 30
Blaier, Blaier, 51
Blau, F. M., 58
  Johann Herman,
  57, 97
Bleyer, Moritz, 97
Boehmker, Howard W.,
  109
Bogenschütz, Karl, 97

118

Boh, John H., 109
Borel, Georg, 22
Bosche, Johan, 97
Böswald, Father Karl, 34
Bouquet, Heinrich, 1, 3
Bowman, Johann 8,
Brake, Nic, 68
Bramlage, Johann
    Gerhard Clemens, 97
Brandlay, Johann, 31
Brecht, John, 69
Brenner, Ms. Friedrich,
    54
    John, 53
Brentle, Michael, 22
Brill, George, 69
Brinkmann, Ms.
    Hermann, 54
Britzwein, Albert, 97
Brons, Dietrich, 31
Brosemer, Karl, 17, 19
Bruner, Joseph A., 32
Brungs, Mary Camelite,
    109
Bruns, Dietrich, 31
Buckner, John C., 4
Bunning, Mrs. Catherina,
    52
Bürkle, Mathias, 30
Busch, Eduard S., 13
    Ernst, 30
    Philipp, 13
Busse, Joseph, 97

Butterfield, C. W., 11,
    109
Butts, Clinton, 15,
    Marshal, 41
Butz, Eduard, 15
Cappel, Joseph, 70
Carlisle, Robert, 16
Carneal, Thomas, 4
Cassel, Daniel Kolb, 12,
    109
Christmann, Jacob, 11
Cole, Arthur C., 38
Collins, Lewis, 11, 12
Conrad, Oskar H., 17
Constanz, Peter, 44
Conzen, Kathleen Neils,
    86
Covington, Gen.
    Leonard, 4
Cronau, Rudolph, 35, 60,
    65, 73, 110
Damal, Jos., 69
Decker, Franz, 30, 31
    Friedrich, 34
Deglow, Henry, 13, 51
    52,
    Herman Rudolph, 97
    Deglow Brewing
    Co., 91
Deisler, Conrad, 51, 97
    Mrs. Conrad, 52
Derbacher, Franz, 23, 33
Deschwanden, Paul, 90
Determann, Lambert, 56

119

Deutenberg, Jos., 69
Dierkes, John, 70
Dietz, Chas., 70
Dinwiddie, Gov., 11
Dölle, Pastor Heinrich,
  34
Donnenfelser, 90
Dorsel, Conrad, 97
Douglass, Paul, 36, 110
Drake, Francis S., 11
Dreesmann, Bernhard,
  29, 98
  Heinrich, 23,
Droege, Ignatius, 98
  Lorenz, 98
Duveneck, Frank, xi, 89,
  94, 95, 98, 109,
  111, 112
Edler, Heinrich, 28
Eduard, Franz, 105
Ehrlenbach, Julius H., 69
Eichler, Moritz, 56
Eifert, Wilhelm, 98
Eilers, Wilhelm, 98
Eisele, Johann, 98
Eisenmann, Christiana,
  34
Endress, Paul, 22
Engert, Adam, 22
  Gustav, 22
  Victor Kaspar, 23,
  51, 96, 98
Ernst, Wilhelm, 29
  William, 93

Faber, Joseph, 30
Falkner, Arnold, 29
Faust, Albert B., 35, 110
Fearsons, Mayor, 43
Feldhaus, Heinrich, 30,
  31
  Hermann, 33
Feldkamp, Franz, 98
Feuss, Wilhelm David,
  98
Fiber, Heinrich, 31
Findsen, Owen, 46, 110
Fischer, Chas., 70
Foley, Mayor, 42, 44
Forbriger, Adolph, 69
Ford, Edward, 12, 110
Fox, Clifford H., 35, 110
Frank, Jacob, 22
Freiberg, Walter A., 110
Freund, Fred, 70
Frey, Doris, 30
Frilling, Fred, 70
Fritz, Felix, 54, 99
Fromann, Paul, 11
Funke, W., 70
Gano, Richard, 4
Gastinger, Henry, 70
Gatenberg, Bernard, 99
Gaubert, Peter, 22
Gausepohl, Bernhard, 31
Gedge, the brothers, 28,
  94
Geiger, C., 69

Geisbauer, Carl or Karl,
    21, 22, 25. 34, 53,
    99
Geiswein, Johann Adam,
    52, 54, 99
    Mrs. Adam, 52
Gensvittle, Bernhard, 22
Gerstle, Gary, 86
Gibb, Bernhard, 31
Giglierano, Geoffrey J.,
    10, 25, 46, 86, 111
Göbel, Pastor, 99
    Wilhelm, 34, 99
Goerdes, Friedrich, 99
Gospole, Karl, 31
Götsch, the brothers, 28
Götz, Fried., 24
    Maria, 32
Greenup, Christopher, 6
Grimes, J. Milton, 79,
    111
Grimm, 90
Grönup, Christopher, 6
Grote, August, 56
Gruenloh, Henry, 70
Günter, Gerhard, 33
Habig, Peter, 30
Haake, Anton, 99
Hagen, Johann, 8
    Valentin, 31,
Haggin, Johann, 8
Hahnhauser, Jacob, 28
Hammann, Heinrich, 30
Hammel, Samuel, 30

Hanekamp, William, 69
Hanhauser, J.G., 23
    Jakob, 22
Hansen, Bernhard, 31
Harding, Jakob, 30
Harmeling, George, 56,
    68
Harrod, Jacob, 7
Harvey, Deputy Sheriff,
    42
Hasemeyer, Johann, 99
Hauser, Frank, 68
Hecker, Friedrich, 40
Heckewelder, Johann,
    116
Heckmann, Friedrich
    Wilhelm, 99
Heermann, Norbert, 111
Hegge, Bernard
    Hermann, 100
    Ernst, 70
Heidel, John P., 68
Heile, Johann Heinrich,
    100
Heimer, Abraham B., 32
Heinzen, Karl, 38
Heiss, Michael, 34
Heit, Abraham, 7
Hellebusch, B. H. F., 51,
    96, 100, 111
Hembrock, Clemens, 30
Henn, Heinrich, 99
Herbst, Lätitia, 30
Herchheimer, Nicolas, 65

Hermann, Fredrich, 31
Hermes, Joseph, 29, 51,
    68, 71, 99
Hewing, Bernard, 101
Hinkson, Johannes, 8
Hite, Abraham, 7
Hoerstling, John C., 71
Hoffmann, Elias, 30
    Jakob, 30
    Johannes, 16
    Wilhelm, 15
Holmann, Jakob, 9
Holtmann, Wilhelm, 100
Höne, Franz, 100
Horstmann, Heinrich, 29,
    30
Huber, Heinrich, 23
Hubig, John, 68
Hudson, John, 4
Huls, C. W., 16
Huntmann, Heinrich, 30,
    31
Hurley, Daniel, 35, 112
Inse, Mathias, 30
Jaegers, Albert, 6
Jäger, George, 6
    Simon, 30
Jakob, Andreas, 31
    Simon, 34
Jonte, Peter N., 22, 23,
    25
Kampe, Georg, 100
Kappel, Johann, 100

Karkadoiulias,
    Elefcherious, 88
Karmann, Johann, 31
Kasing, John, 70
Kennedy, Joseph, 4
    Thomas, v, 6
Kentrup, Heinrich, 100
Kercheval, Samuel, 11,
    112
Kern, Johannes, 14
King, Charles D., x,
Klauprecht, Emil, 12, 47,
    112
Kleinberg, Heinrich, 31
Kleist, Fritz, 100
Klenke, Heinrich, 31
Klette, Louis, 15, 16, 28
Klostermann, Johann
    Bernhard, 82, 101
Klumppe, Joseph Welp,
    68
Knäbel, Simon, 30
Knoll, Franz, 101
Knorr, Georg, 101
Knupfer, Otto, 70
Köbbe, Clemens, 101
Koehnken, A., 90
Koenig, Charles, 70
Koester, Frank, 70
Köhler, Gerog B. F., 101
Korfinghthan, Leonard, 5
Kraft, Adam, 56
Kramer, Heinrich, 31
Kranz, Wm., 69

123

Neuport, Joseph, 23
Niemann, Georg, 23
Nienaber, Ferdinand, 52, 102
Nipper, Bernard Heinrich, 102
Nordhoff, Charles, 20, 113
Norvaski, Alexander, 23
Oaffal, Michael, 20
Oaffel, Michael, 20, 31
Offal, Michael, 20
Osterhaus, 23
Ott, Franziska, 113
Overmann, Heinrich, 23, 31
Pastorius, Franz Daniel, 65
Paul, Conrad, 102
  Johann D., 31
Pendleton, William A., 15
Perdeszet, Friedrich, 17, 19, 23
Pernet, Johann Dietrich, 23
Pershing, Geroge, 75
Pfetzer, Chas., 69
Picot, Johann Christian, 31
Pilcher, Heinrich Ernst, 32
Piper, Johannes, 9

Plumann, Hermann Heinrich, 16
Pohlkamp, Diomede, 113
Prager, Memorial Day, 113
Pumroy, Eric, 113
Puthoff, Herman Heinrich Joseph Puthoff, 24, 103
Rammler, Al, 69
Randolph, Beverley, 3
Rattermann, Heinrich A., ix, 10, 25, 48-50, 52, 113, 115, 116
Rehfuss, Johann, 102
Reich, Stephan, 9
Reichert, Christian, 23
Reichmann, Eberhard, 46, 108
Reisloh, Heinrich, 102
Reitz, John, 70
Renner, Georg Jacob, 102
Riedlin, Ms. Wm. 54, 55, Wilhelm, 56, 57, 68, 91
Riehemann, Ms. H. H., 54
Ries, Louis, 29
Rippley, Lavern J., 46, 108
Rittenhaus, Edmund, 8
  Margaretha, 8

124

Shelby, Isaac, 6
Shinkle, Amos, 13, 93,
    94
    Peter, 13
    Vincent, 13
Siefert, Joe, 19
Sigel, Franz, 66
Silberstein, Iola Hessler,
    35, 115
Smith, Alan Webb, 10,
    115
    Clifford N., 115
Sodowsky, Jacob, 7
    Joseph, 7
Sollors, Werner, 86
Sonntag, Karl, 30
Spanheimer, Mary
    Edmund, 10, 115
Spenneberg, Heinrich,
    104
Stadlaender, Wm., 69
Staggenborg, Frank, 70
    Mrs. B., 54
Stallo, Franz Joseph, 44,
    104
Stängle, Fritz, 56
Stark, August, 69
Staut, Johannes, 104
Stein, Conrad, 104
Stephans, Leonard, 15
Stierlin, Ludwig, 115
Stöckle, Fidel, 104
Stoll, Leonhard, 104
Strader, Johannes, 6

Sträter, Johannes, 6
Strattmann, Wm., 70
Stricker, Sheriff, 42, 44
Supple, Gottfried, 104
Tappert, Fr. William, 90
Taylor, James, 3
    General 29
Teipel, Peter, 105
Tenkotte, Paul A., x, 26,
    115
Terbacher, Franz, 23
Terbe, Johann Wessel, 31
Terlau, Heinrich, 105
Theissen, Heinrich
    August, 105
Thiel, Peter P., 69
Thien, Wenceslaus, 90
Thoss, Franz Eduard, 28,
    105
Todd, John, Jr., 3
Toebben, Matth., 93
Tolzmann, Don Heinrich,
    vii, 10, 11, 26, 35,
    46, 47, 59, 73, 79,
    80, 86, 110, 112,
    114, 115
Trigg, Stephan, 3, 4
Tulleken, Frederich, 3
Tumler, Henry, 69
Uberdick, Dr., 52
Uffal, 20
Ufheil, Michael, 17, 20,
    31

Ulrich, Ernst, 69
  Karl, 105
Unlage, John, 69
Uttenbusch, Wilhelm, 30
Van Hook, Jan, 9
Venken, Heinrich, 31
Vercouteren, Karl J., 76,
  79, 85, 117
Vonderschmitt, Carl A.,
  69
Wachs, Ernst, 70
  Fred, 69
Walker, 22
Walt, Gottfried, 105
Warnke, Heinrich, 105
Warth, Ignatz, 23
Washington, George, 52,
  56, 57,
  Martha, 52
Wayne, Anthony, 5
Wehrmann, Jos., 56
Weinhage, Joseph, 23
Welling, Georg 51, 96,
  105
  Mrs. Georg, 52
  Johann Heinrich, 30,
Wellmann, B. H., 30
Welp, Joseph, 68
Welsh, James, 3
Wendell, Wilhelm, 30
Wendt, Henry, 70
Werking, Johann
  Matthis, 31

Wesemann, Heinrich,
  105
Wiechmann, Anton, 105
Wieschörster, F. H. 56
  G. H., 54,
Willen, Heinrich, 31
  Wilhelm, 24, 105
Williams, Elias, 15
Wimberg, Robert J., 26,
  86, 117
Winter, Johann, 30
Wittke, Carl, 74, 79, 117
Wolf, Daniel, 44
  Karl, 14, 28
Wolff, Alban, 71, 73, 93,
  114, 117
Würth, Johann, 106
Young, Dorothy, x
Zell, Georg, 23
Zucker, A. E., 46, 47,
  117
Zumwalde, Wilhelm, 23
Zwick, G. A., 106

Other books by the author:

www.ingramcontent.com/pod-product-compliance
Lightning Source LLC
Chambersburg PA
CBHW052207270326
41931CB00011B/2262